Gene Trowbridge, ESQ, CCIM
Lake Forest, California

First Edition published 2005

Second Edition published 2007

Third Edition published 2015

Contents

ABOUT THE AUTHOR

Gene Trowbridge, ESQ, CCIM

Lake Forest, California

Gene has been in the commercial and investment real estate business continuously since 1972 and in the legal profession since 1996. As the senior partner in Trowbridge Sidoti LLP, he provides legal and real estate consulting services to individuals and entities, concentrating on the syndication of commercial and investment real estate. He is a member of the California Bar. He has authored several live seminars on group ownership, exchanges, and taxation that have been delivered nationally. His articles have been published in various national real estate publications. He is a frequent speaker on the subject of real estate group ownership at local, state, and national real estate conventions.

Importantly, he has hands-on experience in the syndication business, having been the sponsor of sixteen investment groups and by raising equity from investors through registered representatives in the broker-dealer community. He was responsible for the organization of these investment groups, the acquisition, management, and disposition of the real estate, and the communications with the investors.

Awarded the CCIM (Certified Commercial Investment Member of the CCIM Institute) designation in 1977, Gene continues to serve as a member of the CCIM faculty. In 2002, he was awarded the Robert L. Ward *Instructor of the Year Award* from the CCIM Institute. In 2005, Gene was awarded the Victor L. Lyon Distinguished Service Award for his many years of outstanding contribution to the education program of the CCIM Institute.

Gene invites your inquiry into his consultation and legal services provided by his law firm. He works with real estate professionals throughout the country who are considering entering the group investment business or are already in the business, assisting them with the development and implementation of a strategic plan. Gene offers legal and real estate services to his group investment clients including the formation of the legal entity chosen and the preparation of the Private Placement Memorandum, state and federal securities notices, and all related documents. Complete information on the services provided by the law firm can be found by visiting www.crowdfundinglawyers.net.

Contact Gene at gene@genetrowbridge.com

Gene Trowbridge, ESQ, CCIM
25422 Trabuco Rd., #105-244
Lake Forest, CA 92630-2797
949-855-8399 Voice
949-855-4013 Fax

Gene Trowbridge, ESQ, CCIM

Articles Published and National Speaking Engagements

Regarding Group Investing

Articles

"Group Investing Update" *Commercial Investment Real Estate,* a member publication of the CCIM Institute November/December 2013 http:// www.ccim.com/magazine/

"The Climate for Group Investing" *Commercial Investment Real Estate,* a member publication of the CCIM Institute January/ February 2011 http://www.ccim.com/magazine/

"Group Investing Insights" *Commercial Investment Real Estate,* a member publication of the CCIM Institute September/October 2008 http://www.ccim.com/magazine/

"Tic Talk" *Commercial Investment Real Estate,* a member publication of the CCIM Institute Vol. XXV, NO. 2   September/October 2006 http://www.ccim.com/magazine/

"Group Investing-It's a Whole New Business! (Part 2)" *Professional Report,* a publication of the Society of Industrial and Office REALTORS® Volume 62, Number 3, Summer 2003 http://www.sior.com/publications/publications.html

"Group Investing–It's a Whole New Business! (Part 1)" *Professional Report, a publication of the Society of Industrial and Office REALTORS®* Volume 62, Number 2, Spring 2003 http://www.sior.com/publications/publications.html

"Building a Powerful Portfolio" *Commercial Investment Real Estate,* a member publication of the CCIM Institute March/April 2003 (Contributing Author) http://www.ccim.com/magazine/

"Gaining from Group Investments" *Commercial Investment Real Estate,* a member publication of the CCIM Institute   March/April 2002 http://www.ccim.com/magazine/

Speaking Engagements

Multiple presentations at "Private Money Boot Camps" offered by ReMentor.com

Multiple speaking engagements for Rich Dad, Poor Dad Seminars

Tenant-In-Common Association Symposium, San Diego, CA

Tenant-In-Common Association Annual Conference, Las Vegas, NV

CCIM National Conference, Scottsdale, AZ

Tenant-In-Common Association Annual Conference, Salt Lake City, UT

CCIM National Conference, Reston, VA

CCIM National Conference, San Antonio, TX

CCIM/IREM Commercial Real Estate 2003, Orlando, FL

CCIM National Conference, Chicago, IL

CCIM National Conference, Denver, CO

CCIM National Conference, Reston, VA

TROWBRIDGE CURRICULUM

Online Professional Development Courses

Online Correspondence Courses for State CE Credits

If you like this content, you will also enjoy the professional development courses Gene has developed and the correspondence courses that are available to you as a method of completing your continuing education requirements for renewal of your real estate license.

For the list of courses available, visit **www.trowbridgecurriculum.com**. If your state is not listed for continuing education credits, check back frequently as we are always adding additional states.

FOREWARD TO THE THIRD EDITION

When I wrote the First Edition of *It's a Whole New Business!* I wrote it for the real estate professional who was interested in exploring the opportunities available through the formation of investment groups to acquire, operate, and dispose of investment real estate. I found that the book also appealed to those real estate professionals who have completed several group investments and want to expand their activity in the group investment industry.

In the Second Edition, I expanded certain sections that, through discussions with readers and through interactions with people who attended my workshops, I came to realize were of more interest to my readers than I had originally thought. Through my work in writing private placement memorandums during this period I have also identified the areas that need the most attention when working with new or experienced group sponsors.

Since the publication of the First Edition, the group investment industry has also had some major events, such as the IRS issuing **Rev. Proc. 2002-22** and the National Association of Securities Dealers (NASD) releasing **NASD Notice to Members 05-18** and the passage of **The JOBS ACT.**

Who would have predicted that the tenant-in-common industry would grow to an annual volume some suggest is in excess of $7 billion and then practically disappear? Now, the SEC reports that the volume in the private placement industry annually exceeds $1 trillion with 90% of that volume coming through Regulation D, Rule 506 offerings. Will regulatory crowdfunding ever become law?

In this Third Edition, I have greatly expanded the chapter on securities to include information from the **JOBS ACT** and added a new chapter dealing with **How a Sponsor Can Make Money** in the syndication business.

In the group investment industry, people who form groups are called *syndicators* or *sponsors* and the terms are used interchangeably throughout this book.

In this book, certain Sections of Federal Securities Law and the Internal Revenue Code are included. You will recognize them because the type font will look like this: **IRC Section 1221**

You will see output from a computer analysis of group ownership of investment real estate generated from **planEASe®Windows**. This is the software I use in syndication analysis for clients. For information regarding **planEASe®Windows,** visit their Web site www.planease.com.

> *TIP: Throughout this book, a TROWBRIDGE IMPORTANT TIP (TIP) will appear in this format. These TIPs add my practical insights to the technical material presented.*

Chapter One: It's a Whole New Business!

The Investment Real Estate Process

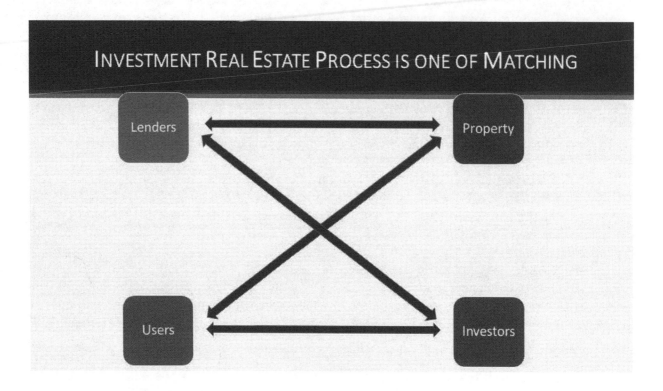

The investment real estate world is a process where, at any one time, several transactions are waiting to happen.

Investors are looking for a property or a property is looking for investors
> At any time, there are investors in the marketplace looking for income-producing properties to purchase. At the same time, there are properties listed for sale in the market that are looking for investors to purchase them.

Properties are looking for users or users are looking for a property
> At any time, there are partially or totally vacant investment properties looking for one or more tenants. At the same time, there may be tenants who are looking for space to occupy in partially or totally vacant investment properties.

Lenders are looking for properties and properties are looking for lenders
> At any time, there are investors looking for lenders to provide debt so they can take advantage of leverage to purchase or improve investment properties. At the

same time there are lenders looking to provide the debt by making loans on income-producing investment properties.

Description of Different Roles

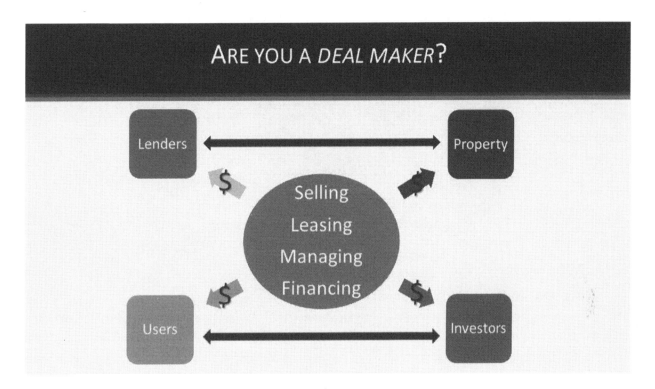

Deal maker and agent

The role of a broker, property manager, or lender, in the real estate marketplace, is that of someone who places themselves in the middle of a transaction occurring in the marketplace. By placing themselves in the middle of these transactions, the broker, property manager, or lender can generate commissions or fees. While taking into consideration the needs of the various clients in the transaction, the actions of the broker, property manager, or lender are essentially that of an agent and are governed by the law of agency. In addition, there may be aspects of fiduciary duty arising from the agency relationship.

Agency law as applied to brokers and agents

An *agent* is one who represents another, the *principal*, in dealings with third parties. Representation of a principal by an agent is called an *agency*.

Agency is the relationship that results from the act of one person, the principal, who authorizes another, the agent, to conduct one or more transactions with one or more third persons. The agent has a duty to exercise discretion in effecting the principal's goals and purposes.

In a typical real estate brokerage contract, an agency relationship is developed between the seller or landlord, who are the principals, and the broker, who is the agent. These agency relationships come in what we call *seller representation* and *landlord representation* assignments.

There can also be an agency relationship created between a buyer or tenant, who are the principals, and the broker, who is acting as their agent. These agency relationships come in what are called *buyer representation* and *tenant representation* assignments.

In addition, dual agency issues arise in commercial and investment real estate when a relationship develops between a broker and two parties in the same transaction with different goals such as the landlord and tenant or the seller and buyer.

The broker-principal relationship may be governed by contract law, agency law, and statutory law.

By entering into a brokerage contract, such as a listing agreement, the principal employs the broker as his or her agent to perform services specified in the contract. The broker is bound to act in the relationship in a manner so as to abide by the provisions of contract law.

In addition to the specific provisions of contract law governing the actions of the broker, agency law provisions would apply. When we enter into a contract to buy or sell a product, we are bound by contract law, but it is unlikely that we have entered into any agency relationship with the other party.

When a real estate broker enters into a contract to provide services to a principal, they must perform their contractual duties within the additional umbrella of the full scope of agency law.

Most states have enacted statutes which require an agent in an agency relationship to act in a certain manner toward the principal. Even in a relationship that does not meet the definition of a contract, it is possible the agent will have established an agency relationship which is governed by statutory law.

For example, generally, an agent's right to be paid a commission and to sue for that commission if it is not paid is based on the existence of a written agreement. There can be, however, an agency relationship created between an agent and a principal without a written contract. An agent, therefore, should be aware that one might owe a duty to a principal whether or not the principal owes a commission to the agent.

Reciprocal
The creation of an agency relationship must be reciprocal. The agency relationship can only be created when it is clear the principal intended to bestow upon someone the status of an agent by giving the agent the authority to represent them, *and* the agent, in return, has accepted that authority.

Formalities
Agency relationships require no special formalities. In an agency relationship, there need not be any written agreement and there need not be any obligation to pay the agent any compensation.

Timing

Conferring the authority in an agency relationship by the principal can take place prior to the actions taken by the agent, or confirmation of the authority can be ratified after the agent has taken the action.

For example, if a real estate agent representing a landlord simply shows a retail tenant a potential location in a strip center, there is no agency relationship created. The agent owes no duty to the potential tenant. But when the tenant asks the agent for specific information such as traffic count, demographics, and competition and the agent provides the information, an agency relationship is likely created. From that point on, the agent has a duty to perform the required agency duties toward the tenant.

Ostensible agency

An ostensible agency may be found to exist to protect third parties who are unaware of the contractual or agency relationships of others. An agency relationship can be found to be created whenever the principal intentionally or unintentionally causes a third party to _believe_ a real estate agent is being used as an agent for the principal.

Scope

The precise scope of an agent's authority in the agency relationship turns on the specific terms of the contract with the principal.

In addition, agents have incidental authority to do everything necessary, proper, and needed in the ordinary course of business to complete the purpose of the agency.

However, there are two limits placed on the powers granted to an agent:
- The agent has no power to execute contracts for the principal.
  Without the principal's express authorization, an agent has no authority to execute a contract on behalf of the principal. An agent's authority to sign contracts for the principal must itself be in writing.
- There are limits on an agent's ability to handle funds.
  The real estate law and regulations of most states severely restrict the manner in which agents may handle funds belonging to their principals. Generally, these funds must be placed in a neutral escrow or trust account.

A list of agency duties in a deal-making capacity

Without going into a complete discussion of agency duties, which is more appropriate in a real estate licensing course, it is important to be reminded of some of the basic duties that occur in an agency relationship. As you read the list, think if you could foresee any conflicts that might arise if you were acting as an agent for a buyer or seller while at the same time operating as the group sponsor of a group that owns a property listed for sale or is in the market to purchase a property.

- Duty of loyalty and good faith
- Duty to be honest and truthful
- Duty to investigate and disclose material facts which might affect the principal's decision
- Duty to disclose the relationship with other party
- Duty to disclose intent to purchase
- Duty to disclose all offers
- Duty of care and diligence
- Duty to disclose profits

Listing agent acts as an intended purchaser

The agency relationship between the broker and principal requires the broker to disclose any material facts that would affect the principal's decision to list the property or sell the property. The broker must not use the agency relationship to obtain any advantage over the principal in any transaction arising out of the agency relationship. The broker must disclose if the broker intends to purchase the property from the principal.

Buyer's broker has an interest in a property

Similarly, a broker representing the buyer must disclose the nature and extent of that broker's direct or indirect ownership of the property, including the broker's membership in a group that has an ownership interest in the property being offered to the buyer. The broker must not use the agency relationship to obtain any advantage over the principal in any transaction arising out of the agency relationship.

An agency relationship may also include a fiduciary relationship

When one person simply employs another person and directs, supervises, or approves the actions of the other person in an agency relationship, it is unlikely that a fiduciary relationship is established. However, when the person employed offers to perform their activity under a relationship of special trust and special confidence involving the exercise of professional expertise and discretion, and the client accepts the offer of these services, a fiduciary duty is established.

It is likely that a fiduciary duty is established in every agency relationship regarding the listing, selling, financing, or management of investment real estate.

Conflicts of fiduciary duties may arise

The issue a group sponsor will face if they choose to enter into the business of group investments while remaining active in deal-making activities is that the group sponsors may be putting themselves in the position of having conflicting fiduciary duties to their clients and their investors.

The Role of a Group Sponsor Is that of a Fiduciary

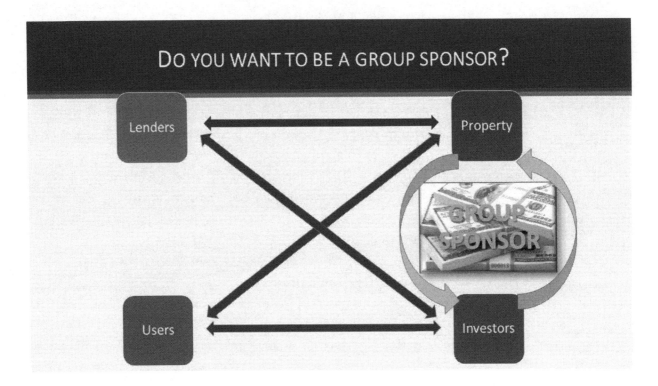

Essentially, the role of group sponsors is to place themselves between the property and the group of investors that owns the property. The flow of money goes from the investors to the property and then from the property back to the investors. The responsibility for managing the group of investors rests with the group sponsor. The reporting of the operations of the property owned by the investment group is also the responsibility of the group sponsor.

The group sponsor need not have any responsibility for the deal-making activities that are normally performed by a real estate agent. The group sponsor need not be a real estate agent. In fact, many who comment on the syndication business suggest the group sponsor should not be a licensed real estate agent so as not to add real estate licensing rules, and the corresponding agency duties to the complexities of the syndication business. Later in this book, we will discuss whether a group sponsor needs to have a securities license.

If a real estate licensee is a group sponsor, as we will discuss later, the combination of these activities will likely create many conflicts that must be understood and addressed by the real estate licensee.

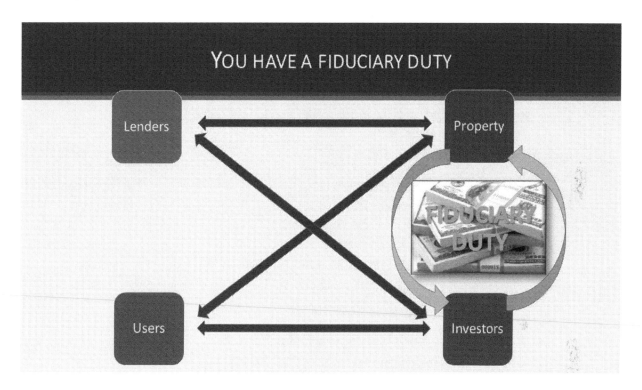

The role of a group sponsor in the ownership of commercial and investment real estate is one of a trustee. The fiduciary duties applied to a trustee go far beyond the duties owed as an agent. The laws relating to a trustee relationship govern the actions of a group sponsor.

Theory of fiduciary duty

The term *fiduciary* comes from civil law and is derived from Roman inheritance practices, where a person who was called a fiduciary, was put in charge of the deceased person's possessions and was charged with the duty of delivering the possessions to the person or persons identified in the decedent's will.

A fiduciary contract exists when one person delivers a thing, such as trust, confidence, or money, to another person on the condition the thing delivered will be returned at some future time. During the time the fiduciary is in possession of the thing belonging to the other person, the fiduciary must act in the best interests of the person to whom the thing must be returned.

When an investor invests in a group owning investment real estate, a contract is formed between the investor and the group sponsor. A fiduciary relationship is established as a result of the investor delivering money to the group sponsor. The group sponsor has a fiduciary duty to the investors in the group. As long as the group sponsor is in possession of the investors' money they must act in the investors' best interests.

Fiduciary duty

A fiduciary duty exists whenever one person, the client, places special trust and confidence in another person and relies upon that person to exercise his discretion or expertise in acting for the client; the fiduciary knowingly accepts that trust and confidence and, as a result, undertakes to act on behalf of the client by exercising discretion and expertise.

Persons who are owed a fiduciary duty have a right to expect the fiduciary will do the following:

- Use their best efforts when acting on the client's behalf
- Not act in any manner adverse or contrary to the client's best interests
- Not act on their own behalf in relation to the client's interests
- Exercise all of the skill, care and due diligence at their disposal on behalf of the client

In addition, a person acting as a fiduciary is required to make truthful and complete disclosures so that informed decisions may be made.

Duty of care

Just as officers and directors of corporations owe a fiduciary duty to their shareholders, group sponsors are required to perform their duties with the care, skill, diligence, and prudence of like persons in like positions.

Group sponsors will be required to make decisions employing the diligence, care, and skill an ordinary prudent person would exercise in the management of their own affairs. This is known as the *prudent investor rule*. This standard is applied to the actions of the group sponsor so as to determine if the group sponsors have performed their fiduciary duties in an appropriate manner.

The *business judgment rule* is the standard applied when determining what constitutes care, skill, diligence, and prudence of like persons in like positions.

This rule does not include the examination of the substantive merits of business decisions of the group manager, but examines

the potential conflicts of interest which were intentionally hidden; or

the failure to follow reasonable procedures such as failure to obtain professional appraisals before selling a property; or

the failure to consider competing offers from potential buyers or potential tenants.

Duty of disclosure

Group sponsors have an affirmative duty to disclose material facts to the investors. It is unlawful for a manager of a group to make an untrue statement regarding a material fact or to omit to tell the investors a material fact.

Information is considered material if there is a substantial likelihood that a reasonable investor would consider it important in making an investment decision.

When members of an investment group are in a position to vote for a major event, the manager of the group must disclose to them the material information needed for them to give informed consent to the suggested action.

Duty of loyalty

Group sponsors have a duty to avoid conflicts of interests. Before raising money from investors, the group manager must disclose any conflicts that may exist between the interests of the manager and the interests of the entire investment group or any of the individual investors.

Group sponsors are restricted from entering into contracts with the investment group that advance the business interests of the manager over the business interests of the entire investment group or any of the individual investors.

Group sponsors may not profit from opportunities which are presented to the manager as a result of the manager's role in the business of the group and are not offered to the group first, regardless of whether the group has the funds needed to act on the opportunity.

Misrepresentation and Fraud

Unfortunately, no discussion of the role of a group sponsor is complete without some discussion of the issues of misrepresentation and fraud. This discussion applies to both the deal-making activities and syndication activities that agents might take if they choose to add the syndication business to their current business. The law is specific in its definition of certain actions or non-actions taken by agents and group sponsors. The courts use these definitions in their analysis of the facts presented, so as to shape the appropriate remedy available to the injured client.

The discussion included here is not meant to be an exhaustive analysis but should serve as a reminder of actions and inactions that may appear to serve one client but end up damaging another.

A common claim of action in a lawsuit against an agent performing deal-making activities in the role of a group sponsor is misrepresentation and fraud. The party claiming injury usually argues that if they had known the facts they would not have invested. They claim the material facts needed to make an informed decision were either misrepresented or concealed from them.

Those who owe an agency duty or a fiduciary duty, as discussed above, must be exceptionally careful not to intentionally mislead the party to whom they owe these duties.

Fraud and deceit through an intentional misrepresentation

Fraud is an *intentional false representation* of a material fact made with the purpose of causing a client to act in a certain way. The client must believe the representation is true and act on the representation, and, as a result, the client must suffer damage. Intentional acts are the most detested and carry the greatest remedy for the party damaged.

Elements of fraud

To prove an action of fraud, it must be shown that

the broker, agent, or group sponsor made some representation as to a past or present material fact; and

the representation must have been false; and

the broker, agent, or group sponsor must have known the representation was false; and

the broker, agent, or group sponsor made the representation with the intent that the client would rely on the representation and act or refrain from acting based on the representation; and the client must have been unaware of the falsity of the representation and acted or refrained from acting based on the representation; and

the client must have sustained financial damage as a result of relying on the false representation.

A defense to the charge of fraud is to successfully show that any one of the above elements was not present.

It is most important to understand that fraud is a crime of *intent*. If intent is absent, fraud is not present.

Examples of intentional misrepresentation

The following is a short list of the types of misrepresentations of which brokers, agents, and group sponsors are likely to be accused.

- Misrepresentation of the value of a property in order to obtain a listing, obtain an offer from a buyer, or to entice an investor to purchase an interest in the group
- Misrepresentation of an ownership interest the agent, broker, or group sponsor has in the property
- Misrepresentation of an agency relationship that exists between the agent, broker, or group sponsor and the property owner, potential buyer, or existing or potential tenant
- Misrepresentation of the condition of a property to the potential buyer, potential tenant, or potential investor made to entice the party to act
- Misrepresentation of the permitted use of a property to a potential tenant or potential buyer to entice the party to act

Fraud and deceit through intentional concealment

Concealment is an *intentional hiding of a material fact* done with the purpose of causing the client to act a certain way. The client must have been unaware of the fact and would not have acted as they did if they knew of the fact, and as a result of acting, the client suffered damage. This is also an intentional act, and the remedies available are substantial.

Concealment

To prove an action of concealment, it must be shown that

the broker, agent, or group sponsor concealed or suppressed a material fact; and

the broker, agent, or group sponsor must have been under a duty to disclose the fact to the client; and the broker, agent, or group sponsor must have intentionally concealed or suppressed the fact with the intent to defraud the client; and

the client must have been unaware of the fact and would not have acted as he did if he had known of the concealed or suppressed fact; and

as a result of the concealment or suppression, the client suffered economic damage.

A defense to the charge of concealment is to successfully show that any one of the above elements were not present. Once again, intent must be present.

Examples of intentional concealment

The following is a short list of the types of intentional misrepresentations brokers, agents, and group sponsors are likely to be accused of.

- Failure to disclose a material fact that would have caused the party to not act on the property
- Failure to explain contingency events properly
- Failure to disclose an existing agency relationship
- Failure to disclose an ownership in the property on the part of an agent, broker, or group sponsor has currently, or will obtain, as a result of an action taken by the client
- Failure to disclose ownership in companies whose services are recommended to the client

Negligence

An act of negligence generally means that brokers, agents, or group sponsors had the duty to perform their job in accordance with the law or industry standards and failed to perform in that way, and as a result of failing to perform in accordance with their duty, the client was damaged. Negligence is not the same as an intentional act, and the remedies or penalties for negligent acts are less severe than for intentional acts.

Those who owe a fiduciary duty as discussed before must be exceptionally careful to perform their duties in accordance with the high standards set by those in the fiduciary industry for the performance of those duties. Those who owe an agency duty must also strive to perform their duty at a level the industry has accepted as a standard of job performance.

Negligence in performance of a duty

A common claim of action in a lawsuit against an agent performing deal-making activities or a group sponsor is negligence in the performance of their duties. The party claiming injury usually argues that if the negligent party had done their job right the party claiming injury would not have been damaged. This claim is that the party owing the duty was the cause of the client or investor's damage due to negligent performance.

To prove a claim of negligence it must be shown that
the party had a duty to act in a certain way; and
the party breached that duty; and
as a result of the breach, the client was damaged.

A defense to the charge of negligence is to successfully show that any one of the above elements was not present.

Examples of negligence in performance of duty
- Not performing management responsibilities to an accepted industry level of performance
- Not providing correctly prepared required reports or documents to the investors in a timely manner
- Not obtaining appraisals at the acquisition and disposition of a property owned by a group
- Not responding to offers on properties owned by the group in a timely manner
- Not remaining current in the market conditions relating to a property owned by a group

Negligence in misrepresentation of the facts
Negligence can also be claimed in the area of misrepresentation of facts. To prove an action of negligent misrepresentation, it must be shown that
the party made a misrepresentation of a past or present material fact; and
the representation must have been untrue; and
the party made the representation, believing it to be true; and
the representation was made with the intent of having the client act in a certain way; and
the client must have been unaware of the false representation; and
the client was justified in relying on the representation and, in fact, acted on the representation; and
as a result of relying on the representation, the client was damaged.

A defense to the charge of negligence misrepresentation is to successfully show that any one of the above elements was not present.

Examples of negligent misrepresentation
- Misrepresentation of current zoning
- Misrepresentation of value
- Misrepresentation of agency relationship
- Misrepresentation of current ownership interest or future ownership interest to be obtained
- Misrepresentation of costs associated with obtaining new financing
- Misrepresenting the financial statements of operations of a property

Can You Perform Agent Activities and Group Sponsor Activities Simultaneously?

Before making the decision to combine the deal-making activities of a real estate agent with the reporting and management activities of a group sponsor, there must be a full assessment of the conflicts of interest that are present when performing both sets of duties.

Assume that your investment group owns an office building that currently has a 7,500 square foot vacant suite. You also have a leasing assignment for a landlord client who has a 7,500 square foot vacant suite. If you find a potential tenant for a 7,500 square foot office suite, which suite do you show them? Do you give the tenant information on what your investment group may provide in the way of incentives or offsets that cannot be given to them by the owner of the property you have listed? If you know that your investment group may accept a lower rental rate than the quoted asking price, can you disclose that to the tenant? How do you tell your landlord client that the tenant has rented the suite in the building your investment group owns and not the suite in their building?

What if you are looking for a property to purchase for an investment group and at the same time you are working your list of property owners to find an investment for an individual investor? When you call on a property owner, are you calling as a potential buyer or a listing agent? How can you handle the apparent competing roles you are undertaking? How will the marketplace accept the dual roles you are playing?

As a broker with licensed agents, how will you handle the fact that your agents hand out their business cards with your company name on them as they look for properties to buy for their investment group or solicit potential investors for the new group they are forming?

While these conflicts may already exist in the life of a real estate agent representing several different clients at one time, you should recognize that these conflicts become more pronounced when you are performing these activities for clients and your investment group simultaneously as a group sponsor.

Can You Fulfill Multiple, Competing Agency, and Fiduciary Duties?

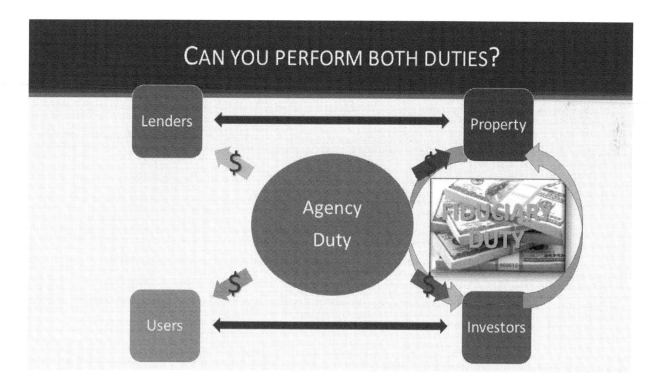

We have already touched on the potential conflicts present when attempting to simultaneously perform the activities of a deal maker and those of a group sponsor as well. Perhaps the more complicated issue is in handling the competing duties you will undertake as a real estate agent and those of a group sponsor.

You are showing a potential user the 7,500 square foot office space listing you have and the vacant space your investment group owns. You know the landlord client will take less for the space than the listed price but will not drop the official listing price. The landlord client will accept an offer that is less than the listed price of your investment group's property. Will you breach your duties if you tell your investment group they need to drop their listing price to compete for this tenant?

You are making a listing presentation of a property the current owner wishes to sell. The owner client has listed the property at your suggested listing price but has told you of some recent business reversals that require them to sell the building quicker, even at a lesser price. Will you breach your duties to the owner client if you suggest to your investment group that it offer less than the asking price for the property?

As a broker, what duties do you have to the landlord client who has the 7,500 square foot vacant space listed with your company through one of your agents who is part of an investment group that owns a building with a similar 7,500 square foot vacant space? What duties do you have to the owner of the property who has listed his property with your company through one of your agents, who is part of an investment group looking to buy similar properties?

A Description of the Syndication Business

The syndication business could simply be described as two activities: pooling resources from multiple investors in an investor group along with providing a layer of management for the investor group. These two activities are not needed if a single investor purchases the property.

Investors provide the equity

Properties are generally purchased with some combination of debt and equity. The property provides cash flow before taxes **(CFBT)**. The lender provides the debt, and in return receives annual debt service **(ADS)**, providing the lender with a return on their money, often stated as the interest rate, and a return of their investment through principal reductions, determined by the amortization schedule.

Investors buy units of ownership in the company and provide the equity needed to purchase the property. In return, each unit receives a portion of the cash flow distribution available from the property. The cash distribution must represent *a return on the investor's equity and a return of* the investor's investment.

Group sponsor takes on risk

Without the requirement of providing any of the debt or equity needed to purchase the property, the group sponsor takes on the responsibility for management of the investment group and assumes the corresponding risk of management. Some group sponsors will contribute equity and actually buy units. This is actually more of a marketing issue than an ownership structure issue as the group sponsor wants to show potential investors that they believe the investment is so attractive they will invest their own money in it. Some call it *having skin in the game.*

As an owner of units, the group sponsor will be paid as an equity investor. But as the group sponsor, the rewards for assuming the risks of group management are fees and profit-sharing arrangements, and the rewards that are only paid because there is someone or some entity providing the management role.

It's a Whole New Business!

Being a group sponsor is actually a business unto itself. As can be seen in the T-bar graphic that follows, the property will produce cash flow before taxes (**CFBT**), the lender will get paid the annual debt service (**ADS**), and the investors will receive cash distribution (**Cash Dist.**) as a result of owning units. In return for the risk (**Sponsor Risk**) taken by providing the management and taking on the fiduciary duties, but without the contribution of debt or equity, the group sponsor will get paid in the form of fees, or percentages of the cash flows (**Fees/%s**), or both.

THE SYNDICATION BUSINESS

	Property	- Debt	- Sponsor	= Investors
0	(Price)	- (Loan)	- (Sponsor Risk)	= ($$/Units)
1	CFBT	- ADS	- Fees/%s	= Cash Dist.
2				
n	SPBT	- Payoff	- Fees/%s	= Cash Dist.
			PV = @ ?%	IRR

The investors pay cash for the units they purchase. The results of their investment may be measured by calculating a yield, such as an Internal Rate of Return (**IRR**). The group sponsor pays nothing for their role as manager or fiduciary and as a result, no yield, such as an Internal Rate of Return (IRR), can be calculated. The benefits the group sponsor receives can best be measured by a present value (**PV**) approach.

Just as the investor makes a decision to invest in units based on the projected returns, when compared to other investment opportunities, the group sponsor must make a decision as to whether to take on the risk associated with fulfilling the management and fiduciary duties in return for the projected rewards from the specific project. The group sponsor must assign a discount rate commensurate with the perceived risk in the investment when calculating the present value (PV) of the future benefits due the group sponsor.

TIP: I have seen group sponsors choose a 15% discount rate to value their position when the property or business opportunity is in a stable position and use a 25% discount rate when the investment is a start-up opportunity or the property is either a new construction project or a repositioning opportunity. You can use these percentages as a rule of thumb, but you should choose your own discount rate based on your perception of risk you will take on as the group sponsor.

Caution: Take care when combining roles!

There are inherent conflicts that arise when one person or entity takes the position of an agent and a trustee in the same transaction. As an agent, the goal is to complete a transaction within the scope of agency laws. The client may ask advice of the agent, and the agent has an obligation to provide advice that meets the acceptable level of professionalism for their particular field. However, it is the client who makes the decision.

As a group sponsor, you will actually make the decisions. The decisions you make will be judged based on a higher standard of practice, including the prudent investor rule and the business judgment rule.

It is the exceptional person who can perform in the role of fiduciary, owing a trustee's loyalty to the investors, and at the same time act as an agent, ignoring the personal goals that an agent has.

Some real estate professionals have decided after facing real, practical, dilemmas that they can perform each of the roles separately but find it too complicated to perform in both functions simultaneously. At that point, some group sponsors give up one of the functions and cease to either group sponsor investments or cease to provide the agent activities the investment group needs performed.

By way of illustration, consider the group sponsor who attempts to perform the role of listing agent on a property owned by the group sponsor's group. As the group sponsor, the duty owed is that of trustee, and the listing agent duty is that of agency. Being placed in the position of losing a commission so the group can get another few thousand dollars may be an uncomfortable one for the group sponsor.

> *TIP: I have seen group sponsors who chose to start their careers by investing their money alongside their investors and agreed to perform all the agent activities at no cost to the group. They often do this as an effort to facilitate the money-raising activity and to be "fair." Their idea was that this approach would eliminate conflicts and reduce costs for the group thereby generating larger profits for each member of the group, including the group sponsor. It is my opinion the group sponsor and the group would be better served if they hired an outside agent who would provide the services and get paid at a market rate.*

Caution: Do not combine deal-maker fees with group-sponsor fees!

Many group sponsors have said the rewards they have received as payment for taking on the risks of being a group sponsor never adequately compensated them for the risks they took. They have said repeatedly the risks encountered were often greater than the rewards received.

Many real estate agents who syndicate a property do so in an effort to earn more fees from what are essentially deal-making activities such as brokerage fees, listing fees, management fees, or financing fees. They see syndication as a way to make more deal-making fees.

Should you take on the responsibility of pooling capital and managing an investment group for a period of five to ten years just to receive a selling commission at the acquisition of the property and a listing commission at the disposition of the property?

If you want to collect more fees from deal-making activities, become better at being involved in deal-making activities! Do not become a group sponsor!

All the deal-making activity fees must be included in the analysis of the operations of *the property* when determining the Cash Flow Before Taxes (**CFBT**) available to pay for the debt and provide a return for the equity provided by the investors who buy units.

Deal-making fees should *never* be included in the fees collected when determining the present value (**PV**) of the position of the group sponsor. Many readers of this book will ignore this advice and will take on the responsibility of a group sponsor to collect fees from deal-making activities. They will not be confident in their ability to ask their investors to pay them for the risks they take on when they agree to manage the investment group and become responsible for the outcome of the investment. Often, first-time group sponsors agree to invest an equal amount of money as the other investors. They just accept traditional fees for the deal-maker activities and agree to do all the other work for free. Why?

It may be because of one of the following reasons:
- They do not know the risk/reward relationship present in syndications.
- They are hesitant to ask their investors (many of whom are family and friends) to pay them for the work they will do.
- Raising equity from individual investors is a new business to them.

- They are worried they will be unable to raise the funds needed to close the transaction quickly and feel they will be more successful if it appears to the potential investors they are working for free.
- "It's the right thing to do!"

> *TIP: I believe acquisition brokerage fees, leasing fees, property management fees, financing fees, and disposition brokerage fees pertain to the operations of the property, not the pooling of capital or the management of the investment group that owns the property. Syndication is a whole new business and should be treated as one with its own profit and loss statement.*

Caution: Conflicts are everywhere!

Later in this book, we will discuss the conflicts that must be disclosed in the offering documents, often called the *private placement memorandum.*

But before we get that far, the commercial and investment agent or broker who is anticipating becoming a group sponsor must consider one very basic conflict.

Have you considered how being both a deal maker and a fiduciary at the same time can affect your existing business? Ask yourself these questions.

Can you represent your group in a leasing activity when another one of your groups owns a competing property with a vacancy? Can you represent your group when your property has a vacancy and at the same time you have a leasing assignment for another client?

Can you still prospect for listings on properties for sale when you are actively buying properties for the groups you are forming? Does the property owner looking to list their property see you as a buyer or an agent?

Can you represent buyers when you are actually competing with them for properties to purchase for your group? Can you represent sellers when you are representing your group in the sale of a competing property?

Can your deal-making activities survive if you turn your attention to group-sponsoring group investments? Can your group investments survive when you must turn your attention to a time-consuming brokerage deal?

If you are the broker or owner of a property management firm, will the people in your company who depend on your deal-making activity for a living understand your new devotion to group investing activities?

If you are an agent working for a broker, does the broker have policies that prohibit you from acting as a group sponsor? If you are both a broker and a group sponsor, will you let your agents group sponsor their own groups?

In the next chapter, we will explore issues you need to address before you decide whether you want to be a group sponsor and enter the syndication business.

> *TIP: Over the years, I have seen different approaches to these conflicts. Some people have chosen not to compete with their clients in their deal-making activities and elected not to become group sponsors. Some have chosen not to compete with their investor partners and have given up deal-making activities for anyone other than the groups they have formed. Some manage their business so they conduct "deal-making" activities and form groups at the same time. Whichever direction you choose, you are better off for having thought through the potential conflicts as you consider being a group sponsor.*

Summary

In this chapter, you have been introduced to a philosophy toward group investing that takes the approach that "It's a Whole New Business!" You must differentiate deal-making activities from the role of the group sponsor. You saw the issues involved with the conflict of agency duties and fiduciary duties. In addition, you were shown a framework to analyze the investor's returns and the returns to the group sponsor. The next question for you to answer is whether you want to be in this "Whole New Business."

Chapter Two: Do You Want to Be in the Syndication Business?

Importance of the Syndication Business

> *TIP: Group investing is often referred to as syndication. The words* group investing *and* syndication *are often interchanged for each other. A syndicate may be defined as a group of people who form an association to undertake a business transaction. Examples of syndications would be buying an insurance policy or buying a ticket on a commercial airline. Individually, we cannot afford to buy the protection offered through the insurance or buy the equipment needed to fly. Through syndication we get access to the product and the professional management of the insurance company and the airline. There are situations where we can only get what we need by pooling our resources with others who have the same goals we have.*

Why Enter the Syndication Business?

The Securities and Exchange Commission estimated that in 2013, more than $1.3 trillion was raised in the US private placement market.

As stated in the previous chapter, the syndication business is different than the business of being a broker, property manager, or lender. Commercial and investment real estate professionals consider entering the syndication business for a number of different reasons.

Desire to generate a new source of current business income

Many commercial and investment real estate professionals enter the syndication business as a result of their desire to generate current income. They believe that by being in this business they will be able to generate listing and selling commissions, leasing commissions, and property management fees.

In reality, the only income that may be specifically generated by being in the syndication business are fees earned for providing services to the investment group and any sharing of distributable cash flow produced in a property owned by an investment group. The commercial and investment professional must realize they can collect the listing and selling commissions, leasing commissions, and property management fees by performing their brokerage functions *without taking on the risk of being in the syndication business.*

The anticipated income to be earned from fees and distributable cash flow must be measured and compared to the anticipated risks taken. A present value (PV) approach can be used to make this comparison. The discount rate chosen must reflect the risk of the specific property or properties to be acquired by the group.

Desire to control properties

By entering the syndication business, many commercial and investment professionals desire to control properties in a way that is more certain than through a buyer's representation agreement, a listing agreement, or a property management contract.

In a typical day in the life of a broker, property manager, or lender, there should be some activities that are devoted to generating new business. Through the syndication business, it is assumed that it is possible to control properties and have the ability to provide the services that lead to the collection of fees without constantly having to constantly prospect for new business.

The tradeoff is that the commercial and investment professional assumes the risks associated with being in the syndication business in return for what appears to be *built-in* future business through the control of properties.

The anticipated income to be earned from this built-in future business must be measured and compared to the anticipated risks taken.

Desire to control clients and their equity

By entering the syndication business, many commercial and investment professionals desire to control clients and their equity in a way that is more certain than through a buyer's representation agreement or listing contract.

Through the syndication business, it is assumed that it is possible to control clients and their equity more certainly than through some contractual arrangement. The tradeoff is the commercial and investment professional assumes the risks associated with assuming the role of fiduciary by being in the syndication business.

The anticipated income to be earned from this control of clients and their equity must be measured and compared to the anticipated risks taken.

Desire to invest in real estate

Many commercial and investment professionals want the same advantages that other investors want from the syndication process: the ability to pool resources and spread risk through diversification of their equity.

Some commercial and investment professionals do not have sufficient equity to control investment real estate by themselves and look to invest with others as a way to accomplish their goals.

Certain brokers and property managers develop relationships with long-term clients and want to invest with them in investment real estate.

Commercial and investment professionals should be aware that many of the benefits they seek from entering the syndication business are established in a contractual relationship between them and the investors, likely found in the operating agreement or partnership agreement. Contracts can be amended and actually nullified, leaving the group sponsor with all the risk and none of the financial benefits.

An example would be the clause in the agreement between the group sponsor and the investors. The group sponsor will be the listing agent on the eventual sale of the property:

Consider the situation where an unsolicited offer to purchase the property is presented by another broker. The investors want to accept the offer, but the offer is not for enough money to pay the group sponsor a listing fee. In fact, the investors do not believe the group sponsor did anything to generate the offer. Most agreements allow a majority of interests in ownership to modify the contract. The investors call for a vote and eliminate the listing commission.

It is not uncommon for an inexperienced broker or property manager to waive their right to a commission on the acquisition of a property by a group of investors, expecting to receive the commission on the disposition of the property. In the example just cited, the group sponsor took all the risks of being in the syndication business and received fewer results than anticipated.

TIP: This situation actually happened to me. In one of my first syndications, I was expecting a commission on the sale of the property. I was doing the ongoing management for free. An unsolicited offer came in that was "only a commission short" of being acceptable to the group. The partners decided to take the offer and not pay me a commission! From then on, my agreements call for me to receive a fixed fee at disposition that is not considered a commission. That fee could always be voted away, but it would take an amendment of the agreement, which is more difficult that having the partners just eliminate the commission.

Advantages to investors

There are many advantages for the investors who choose to invest in groups to purchase commercial investment real estate. Some of the advantages are discussed here:

Ability to purchase a property

The main reason for forming a group of investors to purchase investment real estate is the group's ability to pool resources so that a property may be purchased. Individually, an investor may not be able to complete the purchase, but with pooled equity from several investors, a purchase can be made.

Lack of available financing

During the real estate cycle, there is always a time where obtaining financing for projects is difficult. If the investing world is made up of investors that have 20% equity and, at this time, lenders are requiring 40% equity, it will take two investors to complete a purchase of investment real estate. Forming a group will facilitate the acquisition process.

High prices demand large down payments

There are times during the real estate cycle when the demand for investment real estate is very great and, as a result, the prices on investment real estate rise dramatically. In this situation, a large down payment may be needed so the property can be purchased and generate a positive cash flow.

Generate cash flow

Many investors are interested in investing in a group where a 100% cash purchase is anticipated. In a group with an acquisition strategy of an all cash purchase, the goal will be to generate cash for distribution and eliminate the risk of having debt. Many large public offerings, such as Real Estate Investment Trusts (REITs), are all-cash purchasers of investment real estate, and their results are measured on cash distributions to the investors.

Achieve appreciation

Many group sponsors will form groups with investors who are primarily interested in the appreciation investment properties can provide. Historically, investment real estate has increased in value at a rate faster than inflation. Investors may believe that, in certain stages of the real estate cycle, more appreciation potential exists in larger properties that can be purchased by groups than in the smaller properties they would have to buy themselves if they were limited to their own resources.

Diversification

Many investors join investment groups because they believe it is wise to spread their equity among several investments rather than put "all of their eggs in one basket." They believe in diversification. Instead of an investor putting $1 million into one property on a free-and-clear basis, perhaps the investor would be wiser to diversify into an investment group which is buying two properties free and clear or into another group that is formed to buy four properties using 50% leverage.

Disadvantages to investors

There are also many disadvantages to investors who invest in commercial and investment real estate through group ownership. Some of the disadvantages are discussed here.

Loss of independent decision-making

Many investors feel they lose control of their investment in a group investment. They see this loss of control as a disadvantage. In every group, the decision-making authority will be centered on some individual or some entity over which the individual may have little or no control.

Results can be dependent on the group sponsor

Inherent in a group investment is the concentration of power in an individual or entity other than the individual investor. Decisions must be made on a daily basis. The results of the decisions made by the group sponsor may be positive or detrimental to the eventual outcome of the investment.

Investor's objectives may change

Real estate is by nature a long-term investment. It is possible that, during the life of the investment, an individual's investment goals may change. When the change in goals takes place and the investor's money is tied up in a group investment, the investor may be unable to free up needed capital in a timely manner to meet the changing objectives. A person planning to be a group sponsor of a group investment needs to know that an investor such as this may become a problem for the group sponsor and for the group. Planning for a solution to this problem is imperative, and the terms of the operating agreement or partnership agreement must address this.

Lack of liquidity and marketability

Real estate by nature is an illiquid investment. Loss of liquidity is the risk associated with the inability to convert an investment to cash without a loss in principal. Selling an interest in a group investment prior to the dissolution of the group almost always results in a discount from the market value of the investment.

Marketability is another enumerated risk associated with the inability to convert an investment to cash at any price. Group sponsors must be aware there may not be a market for the sale of units in the group they are forming unless their group's operating agreement specifically addresses this issue. The investor should be aware that even with the existence of a provision for marketability they may not be able to sell their units at the price they want at the time they want to sell!

Group sponsor's financial position may change

Group sponsors of group investments often sponsor numerous investments but have limited resources. Some investments may not work out as planned, and the group sponsor may be required to or may volunteer to commit substantial resources to one group. It is possible the expenditure on behalf of one group may be at the expense of the group sponsor's ability to help other groups.

Three areas of activity not requiring the broker to be a group sponsor

There are three deal-making activities where an agent or broker could become involved in the syndication business but would not require the broker or agent to become a group sponsor.

Acquisition

You could become involved in the acquisition of investment real estate by groups without becoming a group sponsor. Many group sponsors are looking for property to purchase and count on real estate professionals to introduce them to properties where the economic benefits fit the group's investment objectives. The Certified Commercial Investment Member (CCIM) Institute offers educational courses that prepare the real estate professional for the tasks of evaluating the acquisition, ownership, and disposition of investment real estate. The CCIM Institute grants the CCIM designation to individuals who complete stated educational and experience requirements. Find out more about the CCIM Institute at their Web site www.ccim.com.

Management

You could become involved in the management of investment real estate groups without becoming a group sponsor of a group. Many group sponsors are looking for property managers to handle the daily operations of the property their group owns. IREM, the Institute of Real Estate Management, offers practical educational courses covering the management skills real estate professionals need to properly manage investment real estate. IREM grants the CPM (Certified Property Manager) designation to individuals who complete stated educational and experience requirements. Find out more about IREM at their Web site www.irem.org.

Disposition

You could become involved in the disposition of real estate owned by investment groups without becoming a group sponsor. Many group sponsors are looking for real estate professionals to help them dispose of real estate the group owns.

> *TIP: The real estate professional looking to provide these services to an investment group should be certain the person who is going to sign the purchase agreement, the management contract, or the listing agreement on behalf of the group actually has the authority to bind the group into a contractual relationship. The best way to be certain of the authority of the person(s) with whom you are dealing is to see a copy of the document that gives the person(s) the authority to bind the group to a contract.*

Three general types of syndications

There are three general types of syndications identified in this business: fully specified, semi-specified, and blind pool. Each type of syndication has its own characteristics.

Fully specified

A fully specified syndication is one where all the real estate the group will own is identified prior to any money being raised from the investors. This is the most common type of syndication found in the marketplace. Often a fully specified offering is limited to one property. For example, a specified offering would be an offering where a group is being formed to raise money to buy a specified apartment building or a specific industrial building.

Semi-specified

A semi-specified offering is when some of the properties to be acquired are specifically identified, but additional money may be raised from the group members so the group can buy other properties that become available.

Generally, a semi-specified offering has a specific acquisition strategy that is followed by the group sponsor. Semi-specified offerings are often within one property type. For example, a group may be formed to follow the acquisition strategy of purchasing foreclosed office buildings direct from the reacquiring lenders. One building is identified, the money is raised, and the building is obtained. Then with the additional money raised, the group will search for another acceptable foreclosure property to purchase.

Blind pool

In a blind pool, the group is formed and the group members invest their money before any specific properties are identified. The acquisition strategy of the group should be well-defined. An example of a blind pool acquisition strategy would be to purchase triple net leased properties in a specific geographic area, with capitalization rates not to be less than 7%, where the tenant has an AAA credit rating.

Blind pools can be very large in terms of the amount of money raised and the number of investors involved in the group. Because many investors may be involved, these offerings will likely be a public offering, such as a Real Estate Investment Trust (REIT). Blind pools usually require registration under the securities laws because the group sponsor may have to resort to using advertising and general solicitation to find the large number of investors needed.

TIP: Investors should carefully study the acquisition strategy of the group in which they are planning to invest. Most investors would feel that a fully specified offering would be less risky than a blind pool. Only the most experienced group sponsors can expect to attract investors' capital into a blind pool.

Other Considerations

There are other considerations that must be examined when deciding to become a group sponsor of group investments in real estate.

The group sponsor must be aware of legal and security considerations

When real estate professionals decide to become group sponsors of a group investment, they enter a new area of legal considerations and a new area of securities laws. The potential group sponsor does not need to be afraid of unfamiliar legal and security law aspects of group investing but should know how and when these considerations will affect them.

The group sponsor will need an attorney and a certified public accountant (CPA)

As a group sponsor, it will be important to work with an attorney who knows how the state and federal laws relate to the formation of the entity. The attorney must also know securities law on both the federal and state level.

A CPA will be needed to give the group sponsor advice regarding federal and state income tax laws and how decisions of the group sponsor will affect the investors in the group. In addition to understanding the tax laws, a CPA will be needed to prepare the annual accounting for the group and prepare the information that must be distributed annually to the members of the group.

The group sponsor needs to understand the lending rules that apply to group ownership

Lenders will have specific requirements regarding those persons or entities who can sign on the loan. The group sponsor will generally sign for the group. The group sponsor must understand whether they will assume any liability when they sign the loan documents. Lenders may require a personal guarantee from each member of the group, or just those who own more than 20% of the group, or just the group sponsor, or no personal guarantees may be required.

The group sponsor needs to understand the rules of the Internal Revenue Code (IRC)

Many questions asked about syndication are not really questions about the legal structure of the entity or the effect of the securities laws but are questions that relate to the IRC. The group sponsor needs to be aware of and understand the application of the rules in the IRC.

The group sponsor needs to understand the long-term nature of the relationship being formed with the group members

Becoming involved with group investments requires a commitment to a long-term relationship with investors. Investment real estate generally requires a long-term hold, and the group sponsor is going to be involved with the group for the entire holding period. Investor's goals may change, just as the group sponsor's goals may change, but the group sponsor must remain with the group.

Groups may remain together after the holding period of the property. This may occur when the group sells the property, in a time in the real estate cycle when financing is not available, and the group carries part of the financing for additional years.

It is not uncommon for a group's legal documents to require the group sponsor to keep financial statements for the six most recent fiscal years and keep the entire books and records of the group for the past three years. The retention of these records by the group sponsor is needed to provide the group and the individual investors with information needed for events such as tax audits, lawsuits, and estate planning.

> *TIP: An investor who had purchased a $25,000 unit in a group designed to develop and hold two mini-storage projects called me to say that she needed her money back because her son's car needed a new engine and transmission. Her goals had changed. Unfortunately, the investment group's rules did not have a provision that allowed for the liquidity she needed. What plans have you made for the investor who suffers the loss of a spouse, a divorce, a bankruptcy, or other financial emergency and needs to liquidate the investment in your group?*

Investment goals must match

In a successful group investment, the goals of all the parties start out the same and remain the same throughout the life of the investment.

Clearly state the goals

The reason for forming the group must be clearly stated in terms that can be understood by each investor. It is important the goals of the individual investor match the goals of the group being formed. It is also important the goals of the group sponsor match the goals of the group.

Match potential investor's goals with property benefits

Investment real estate can produce a number of benefits. Each investor should be made aware of the benefits anticipated from the investment being made. The benefits can be described by using the acronym IDEAL.

I	stands for	income the property produces that can be distributed to the investors in the form of annual cash distributions.
D	stands for	depreciation the property produces that can be used to shelter the income the property produces that is distributed to the investors in the form of annual cash distributions. Some investors need the depreciation an investment produces to offset the income being produced from other, unrelated investments. Brokers, property managers, or lenders considering entering the syndication business should have an understanding of the depreciation provisions and the passive loss rules of the Internal Revenue Code.
E	stands for	equity build up the property produces through the pay down of principal through the amortization of the mortgage.
A	stands for	appreciation the property produces through an increase in value. Appreciation may come from the increases in income the property produces over time or from value-enhancing activities such as remodeling, expansion, or changing the use of the property.
L	stands for	leverage available through the use of financing. Positive leverage exists when the after tax cost of funds is less than the after tax unleveraged yield of the property.

Choose a property type or choose an investor type

As a result of completing the Preconsulting Questionnaire and then proceeding to the second phase of the strategic planning process, it becomes apparent the person considering entering the syndication business will need to know whether their first investment group will be based on a product type or investor type.

Investors desire certain economic benefits

Certain groups of investors will want certain benefits and not be interested in others. For example, retired investors would likely be more interested in the I (income) the investment produces than the D (depreciation) the property produces. A group of investors interested in cash flow and worried about loss of principal may want to use less L (leverage) in their investment strategies.

If the group sponsor makes a decision that the market for their product is centered in a particular group of investors, the group sponsor will then find the property type that produces these benefits. It is likely that retail or industrial properties with long-term tenants, produced with a low level of leverage, would be the type of property that would need to be owned by a group of retired investors.

Property types produce certain benefits

Each of the four basic product types—industrial, office, retail, or multifamily—produces a specific set of benefits. For example, long-term leases present in retail and industrial properties provide strong *I* (income) but not a high level of *A* (appreciation). Multifamily properties generally are considered to be a property type that produces a high level of *A* (appreciation) and are purchased using higher levels of *L* (leverage) than other products types but produce little *I* (income) for distribution.

If the group sponsor makes the decision that the market for their product is a specific property type, perhaps because of their brokerage experience, the group sponsor will then have to concentrate their marketing efforts on identifying and attracting the investor group that looks for the benefits which are expected to be generated from that product type.

Summary

As every experienced group sponsor will tell you, there is a tremendous amount of documentation, management, and administration needed to complete a real estate transaction completed through a group ownership whether it is an LLC or TIC.

Working with lenders, obtaining state and federal securities clearances, and issuing investor certificates make one transaction with ten investors seem like ten separate transactions that all have to close at the same time!

In this chapter, you were exposed to the advantages and disadvantages of group investing, both from the investor's viewpoint and from the group sponsor's viewpoint. In the next chapter, we will see that if you choose to continue exploring this business, the first question you will have to deal with is the entity structure you will need to work under as "It's a Whole New Business!"

Chapter Three: Understanding Tenant-in-Common Interests

Tenant-in-common interests

The first question a group sponsor must ask when contemplating forming a group is whether their potential investors will require the benefits of tax deferral on the acquisition or disposition of the planned investment. Tax deferral can be accomplished through the use of the IRC Section 1031. However, one of the basic aspects of the tax deferral available through a Section 1031 exchange is that only real estate equity can be exchanged. This presents a problem for a group sponsor in that interests in a partnership, which include interests in an LLC, are not eligible for tax deferral because they do not represent real estate equity. Therefore, we need to discuss the availability of using tenant-in-common interests when forming a group, as each tenant-in common will have a fractional deed representing real estate equity.

Tenant-in-common (TICs)

One of the easiest ways to facilitate the pooling of resources for the ownership of commercial or investment real estate would be for two or more investors to invest the needed equity to purchase a property and take title to a partial deed, referred to as *fractionalized* interest in the property as a tenant-in-common.

Throughout this discussion, you will see the importance of two overriding issues.

First, the sponsor must be certain the grouping of investors in a TIC arrangement is done properly so as to ensure the availability of tax deferral under IRC Section 1031, on both the acquisition and disposition of the individuals' fractionalized interests.

Secondly, the sponsor must be certain the grouping of investors in a TIC arrangement is done properly within the rules of the securities industry, under the supervision of the SEC, so the investors' equity can be raised in accordance with the rules associated with using licensed registered representatives through the security industry or by using licensed real estate agents through the real estate industry.

Not a legal entity but a combination of fractionalized interests

Ownership of investment real estate by two or more investors who take title in a properly structured TIC is not ownership by a legal entity but is simply the ownership of fractionalized interests in real estate by multiple investors.

The title to property owned by two investors, one investing 60% and the other investing 40%, may read: to "A" as an undivided 60% interest and to "B" as an undivided 40% interest. Each member holds direct real estate title to their individual interest through a separate deed. Holding direct title to real estate is a prerequisite for completion of a tax deferred exchange under the terms of IRC Section 1031. The availability of a tax deferred exchange has been a primary reason for the current popularity of tenant-in-common ownership programs.

All ownership interests manage their own investments

Each owner of a TIC interest must be in a position to make all of the management decisions in relation to their individual interest. Decisions on acquisition, operations, financing, and disposition of the property must be made by each owner of a TIC interest.

The property stands for all the liability

Each TIC interest may incur liability for any action that occurs on the property. The property could actually be sold by order of the court through a partition action in an effort to satisfy a liability incurred by one of the tenants-in-common. In addition, as a result of events such as death, divorce, and bankruptcy of one of the tenant-in-common owners, the court could require the entire property be liquidated to satisfy a legal remedy.

Each ownership interest reports their individual income tax results

At the end of the year, the owner of a TIC interest would be presented with an accounting for the entire operations of the property. Then the taxpayer will report a share of operating income, operating expenses, and interest expenses in the same percentage as their ownership percentage in the property. Each TIC interest could have their own cost basis and will determine their individual deduction for cost recovery. Any application of the passive loss rules discussed in the chapter on income tax and accounting will be applied to the individual tax return of the TIC interest.

TIC interests and IRC Section 1031

The first issue in the formation of group ownership using TIC interests is whether the IRS will consider the arrangement to be a *business entity*, and therefore a partnership, rather than direct ownership in real estate. If it is determined that a business entity exists, the asset the investor owns will be classified as a partnership interest, not real estate. Partnership interests are not eligible for tax deferral under IRC Section 1031.

IRC Section 1031

The language of IRC Section 1031 is quoted as:

Sec. 1031. Exchange of property held for productive use or investment
STATUTE
(a) Nonrecognition of gain or loss from exchanges solely in kind
(a)(1) In general
No gain or loss shall be recognized on the exchange of property held for productive use in a trade or business or for investment if such property is exchanged solely for property of like kind which is to be held either for productive use in a trade or business or for investment.
(a)(2) Exception
This subsection shall not apply to any exchange of
(A) stock in trade or other property held primarily for sale,
(B) stocks, bonds, or notes,
(C) other securities or evidences of indebtedness or interest,
(D) interests in a partnership,
(E) certificates of trust or beneficial interests, or
(F) choses in action.

IRC Section 1031, (a)(1) states the taxpayer, desiring to achieve tax deferral, *must dispose of real estate* that was held as a trade or business or investment property *and acquire real estate* the taxpayer intends to use as a trade or business or investment property. This is discussed more fully in the chapter on income taxes and accounting issues.

IRC Section 1031 (a)(2) lists assets that are specifically exempted from the tax deferral offered from this Section. As can be seen, exception (D) is stated as *interests in partnerships*. This exclusion was added in 1984. Although a partnership or limited liability company can complete an exchange at the entity level, the individual investor's partnership interest or membership interests are excluded from tax deferral under Section 1031.

If a broker or agent is interested in using the TIC ownership strategy as a vehicle for pooling resources, they should consult with their attorney regarding the current approach the IRS is taking toward the formation of TICs in a way that will allow the investors to take advantage of tax deferral.

IRS Revenue Procedure 2002-22

The IRS was overwhelmed with requests

Pooling of resources through TIC structures has always been available. In 1999, as properties were appreciating and sellers were looking to defer the tax on capital gains, the popularity of these TIC transactions grew. Many TIC sponsors contacted the IRS with requests for private letter rulings that would establish that a particular structure would not be deemed a partnership. The sponsors would describe their structure to the IRS and ask the IRS to rule on whether their structure would be deemed a partnership. Sponsors had few guidelines, and the IRS was overwhelmed with these requests. In 2000, the IRS actually issued a revenue procedure telling sponsors to stop requesting letter rulings.

This situation was unacceptable

Leaders in the TIC industry met with the IRS over a two-year period, requesting the IRS provide guidelines that sponsors could look to in their efforts to properly structure their TIC.

IRC Revenue Procedure 2002-22

In March 2002, the IRS released Revenue Procedure 2002-22 which addressed the issue of undivided or fractional TIC interests as related to IRC Section 1031. It is important the real estate broker or agent who has chosen a TIC structure in which to operate understands the implication of this ruling. The sponsor has a duty to investors to do everything possible to assure the TIC structure will be structured so that the tax deferral desired is available to the investors.

While the complete text of Revenue Procedure 2002-22 is beyond the purpose of this book, a discussion of its major points follows.

Guidelines for a request for ruling

If a sponsor wants to ascertain as to whether a TIC structure will qualify investors for tax deferral under IRC Section 1031, the sponsor could request the IRS issue a ruling on the specific structure of the group.

Section 5 of Revenue Procedure 2002-22 outlines the information that must be submitted with a request for a ruling. All of the following must be included:

- The name, taxpayer identification number, and percentage interest of each co-owner
- The name, taxpayer identification number, ownership of, and any relationship among, all persons involved in the acquisition, sale, lease, and other use of the property, including the sponsor, lessee, manager, and lender
- A full description of the property
- A representation that each of the co-owners holds title as tenants-in-common under local law
- Promotional documents relating to the sale of the tenant-in-common interests
- Financing documents
- Agreements among co-owners
- Any lease agreement
- Purchase and sale agreement
- Any property management or brokerage agreement
- Any other relevant information

As can be seen from the list above, the IRS generally does not issue rulings on hypothetical deals, only real deals.

Conditions for obtaining a ruling

The IRS lists sixteen conditions they want to see in a TIC structure to differentiate it from a partnership interest. They are briefly described as follows:

1) Each of the co-owners must hold title to the property as tenants-in-common under local law.

As such, there can be no entity created, just a group of owners each having a direct ownership interest in the real property.

2) The number of co-owners must be limited to no more than thirty-five persons (a husband and wife are treated as a single person for this purpose).

This condition limits the number of fractionalized interests that can be owned by investors.

3) The co-owners may not file a partnership tax return or otherwise hold themselves out as a partnership or other form of entity.

This is another condition that distinguishes a TIC structure from a partnership.

4) The co-owners may enter into a limited co-ownership agreement that may run with the land.

"Running with the land" may mean there is a deed restriction granted by each of the individual deed holders. This agreement may provide that the co-owner must offer their interest for sale to the other co-owners at a fair market value before exercising any right of partition. The agreement may also provide for majority voting on certain issues.

5) The co-owners must retain their voting rights to require unanimous approval for any sale, lease, or re-lease of a portion or all of the property, any negotiations, or renegotiations of negotiation of any management contract. The co-owners may agree to a majority approval on all other actions.

It is generally understood that this condition means the owners may, at any time, without cause, vote to terminate any management agreement that involves the property. Group sponsors should be concerned about this clause if they are creating this group primarily to generate fees from contractual agreements with the individual owners.

6) Each co-owner must have the right to transfer, partition, and encumber their interest in the property without the agreement or approval of any person.

Restrictions that are required by a lender that are consistent with customary lending practices are not prohibited. Often the lenders place limits on the ability of the individual owners to do what they wish with their interests while the lender has a security interest. Some lenders require the sponsor be allowed to remain in a contractual relationship with the owners or the loan will be deemed to be default. This lender requirement does limit the ability of the individual to do whatever they want with their property, but, since these limits are imposed by the lender and not the sponsor, it meets the conditions imposed by the IRS.

7) Upon sale of the property, any debt secured by the property must be satisfied and the remaining proceeds distributed to the co-owners.

This condition limits the ability of the sponsor to collect some share of the sales proceeds as they might in a limited liability company.

8) During operations, each co-owner must share in all revenue and expenses associated with the property in proportion to their interests in the property.

9) Neither the other co-owner, sponsor, nor manager may advance funds to a co-owner to meet expenses associated with the property, unless the advance is recourse and is not for a period exceeding thirty-one days.

This condition limits the ability of a sponsor lending money to any owner as would be allowed in a limited liability company.

10) The co-owners must share in any indebtedness secured by the property in proportion to their undivided interests in the property.

This condition can be troublesome when the sponsor needs to obtain the financing and must stay liable on the note, even when the sponsor has no ownership interest in the property.

11) A co-owner may issue an option to purchase his interest at fair market value and may not acquire an option to sell the interest to the sponsor, the lessee, another co-owner, the lender, or any person related to such parties.

This condition limits the TIC structure from having the ability for the sponsor to purchase interests from the individuals at discounted prices as is often present in limited liability companies. Liquidity in TIC structures is a common concern of potential TIC investors and, while the industry is relatively new, it is anticipated the sponsors of TIC offering will be involved in providing liquidity to their investors in some manner.

12) The activities of the co-owners must be limited to those customarily performed in connection with the maintenance and repair of rental real estate.

This condition means the TIC entity cannot run a business like a hotel but could own the hotel property and lease out the operations to a hotel operator.

It also may limit a TIC entity from taking the position of a developer of real estate to be sold to others.

13) The co-owners may enter into management or brokerage agreements which must be renewable no less frequently than annually. The manager or broker may be a sponsor or co-owner but not a lessee. The manager may not be paid a fee based in whole or part on the income or profits derived from the property and the fees may not exceed the fair market value of the manager's services based upon comparable fees paid to unrelated parties for similar services.

This is a problematic area for many sponsors who are syndicating to receive fees from what we called *deal-making activities* in the first chapter.

14) All leasing agreements must be bona fide leases for federal tax purposes. Often, in multitenant properties, the sponsor will master lease the property from the TIC owners. This master lease must be at market value and not give an economic advantage to the sponsor.

15) The lender may not be a related person to any co-owner, the sponsor, the manager, or any lessee of the property.

This condition limits the ability of the sponsor or any TIC owner from lending money to another TIC owner as may be allowed in a limited liability company.

16) Payments to the sponsor for the acquisition of the co-ownership interest and services must reflect the fair market value of the interest acquired and the services rendered. The payments of fees may not depend, in whole or in part, on the income or profits derived from the property. No back-end or carried interest is permitted to be paid to the sponsor.

This condition really differentiates the fees that may be paid to a sponsor in a TIC transaction from the fees paid and distribution of cash flow made to sponsors that is usually a part of a limited liability company.

Sponsors have the responsibility to comply

Sponsors who are interested in forming groups using tenant-in-common interests must adapt their programs to conform to the conditions listed above to protect their investors' ability to achieve the tax deferral they desire.

Not a *safe harbor*

It is worth paying special attention to Section 3 of this revenue procedure:

Section 3. scope

This revenue procedure applies to co-ownership of rental real property (other than mineral interests) (the Property) in an arrangement classified under local law as a tenancy-in-common. ***This revenue procedure provides guidelines for requesting advance rulings solely to assist taxpayers in preparing ruling requests and the Service in issuing advance ruling letters as promptly as practicable. The guidelines set forth in this Revenue Procedure are not intended to be substantive rules and are not to be used for audit purposes.*** (Emphasis added)

Section 3 causes prospective sponsors concern. It clearly states the reason for the Revenue Procedure is only to provide guidance in submitting requests for a private letter ruling from the IRS. It also states the sixteen conditions are not to be relied upon by the sponsor in the event of a subsequent audit.

In practice, very few sponsors apply for the private letter ruling. TIC agreements are drafted and the investors are given a disclaimer informing the investor that the only way to be certain that a TIC agreement meets the requirements of the IRS is to obtain the private letter ruling. The group sponsor will tell the investors that they are not going to get the letter ruling, and the tax deferral from the exchange is at risk in the event of an audit.

The current issue is that the Revenue Procedure does not give the sponsor or the sponsor's attorney the ability to say the structure, even following the sixteen conditions listed, will definitely provide the investors with the structure they need for tax deferral. Few lawyers will find that the Revenue Procedure will provide the basis for them writing an opinion stating the structure *will* stand up under an audit. Perhaps more attorneys will be comfortable in writing a *should* opinion. In the current state of the industry, there is some amount of risk associated with the structure of TIC offerings. The sponsors should advise potential TIC investors and their advisors of this risk, prior to accepting a TIC investor's funds.

TIC interests and securities laws

As will be discussed in the chapter on securities laws, an investment that is considered to be an investment contract is deemed to be a security under the federal securities laws. If an investment contract is found to exist, the sale of a TIC interest would be deemed to be the sale of a security. If a commission is paid on the sale, a licensed registered securities representative must be involved.

If, on the other hand, no security interest is being sold in a TIC transaction and a commission is paid, only a licensed real estate agent need be involved in the sale.

Current structures

Currently, a majority of public TIC sponsors are offering investment interests in their TIC transactions as securities through NASD members who are licensed securities agents. These sponsors have set up the TIC arrangement so that, while it is designed to follow Revenue Procedure 2002-22 for IRS purposes, they have retained enough control over the investment they believe it could be determined their efforts are enough to meet the fourth prong of having the profits occur *through the efforts of others*.

If a broker or agent is interested in using the tenant-in-common ownership strategy as a vehicle for pooling resources, they should consult with their attorney regarding the current approach the SEC is taking toward the formation investment groups, using tenant-in-common ownership interests as they relate to state and federal securities rules.

Common questions related to LLC structures

Two of the most common questions I get relate to TICs and LLCs at formation and at the time of the sale of a property. While the answers are quite detailed, a brief discussion is warranted.

At formation

This question goes something like, "I have an investor who has money coming out of a 1031 exchange and wants to invest in our LLC. Can we take their money?" Unfortunately, the answer is almost always no.

The reason for that is found in the requirement that the exchange must involve real estate equity given up for real estate equity acquired. Interests in an LLC are not real estate; they are partnership interests and, therefore, the investor cannot acquire them and achieve their goal of tax deferral.

At disposition of a property

This question goes like, "We have an LLC that is selling a property, and one of my investors wants to take their proceeds and exchange them for another property through a tax deferred exchange. Can they?" Unfortunately, most of the time the answer is no.

The reason is basically the same. What one individual investor in an LLC owns is interest in the LLC, which is not real estate equity. So the individual investor owns nothing that can be exchanged with tax deferral.

You should take note that the LLC, which has title to the property, could do a tax deferred exchange, and it would be done with least complications if all of the investors stayed in the LLC going into the next property.

Drop and swap

There is a strategy that is commonly called *drop and swap* that could be explored with the help of a CPA or tax attorney. Basically, it requires the LLC at some time prior to the actual sale of the property to dissolve and distribute ownership of the property to all the investors through fractional interests to establish a TIC ownership. That is what the word *drop* signifies. *Swap* stands for the process that the individual tenants-in-common would take to complete a tax deferred exchange.

Why is that complicated? First, the new TIC structure must be established in a way that comports with the Rev. Proc. 22-2002 so that the new structure is not determined to be a partnership, which would negate the ability to complete a tax deferred exchange, and, therefore, nothing would have been accomplished.

Secondly, the new TIC group cannot accomplish anything unless each individual owner agrees. Everything needs to be conducted with unanimous approval, which complicates the transaction.

Lastly, according to the Rev. Proc. proceeds from the sale of the property can only be distributed to the individual tenant-in-common owners. That precludes the sponsor from receiving any compensation at the time of the sale.

A transaction that includes distributing the interests from an LLC into a tenant-in-common ownership and then allowing each individual to complete a tax deferred exchange can be accomplished, but it takes planning, the involvement of a tax professional as an advisor, and time to implement.

Future of the TIC industry

   Tax treatment of TICs and Sec. 1031 exchanges

   During the summer of 2006, the TIC community got a real scare from Congress as the tax writing committee considered whether to eliminate Section 1031 treatment for TIC transactions. As the issue of tax deferral is the main driver in the popularity of exchanges and exchanges have been fueling the TIC market, the elimination of tax deferral for TIC interest would be a drastic blow to the industry.

   Senator Grassley (R-IA), then Chairman of the Senate Finance Committee, suggested that eliminating Section 1031 treatment for TIC investments would be a revenue-raising idea for the government. The Senate Finance Committee believed the tax deferral, or as they put it *lost revenues*, were becoming a serious issue and the trend was for more deferrals in the future.

   While the Senate version of the tax bill presented to the Reconciliation Committee included the TIC proposal, the House version of the bill did not. The final version of the bill did not include the provision for the TIC proposal.

   The questions that many industry and Washington observers are asking is was this TIC proposal just an aberration, or will the need to find revenue enhancers in the future once again focus the spotlight on TICs?

Proposed legislation

   Since 2006, every year there have been proposals in front of Congress that will repeal or limit tax deferral through Sec. 1031 exchanges. The group sponsor would be wise to follow the progress of any current legislation in this area.

Summary

When the first edition of this book was published, there were only four pages devoted to tenant-in-common ownership. When the first workshops in support of the book were presented, practically no time was spent on TIC transactions. The landscape of the group investing world changed in 2002 and reached a hectic pace in 2005 and has subsequently slowed as the real estate industry saw equity being wiped away through the difficult times from 2007 to 2012. With decreasing equity, there is likely decreasing taxable gain to be deferred and the volume of exchanges decreased.

However, in the last few years, values have increased, and taxable gains have returned, increasing the volume of exchange transactions. Today, the topic of tenant-in-common demands an hour or more of the time spent the first morning of our workshops. The professional interested in sponsoring groups should continue to monitor the process of the TIC industry as "It's a Whole New Business!" inside the group sponsor business.

In the next chapter, we will examine the more common methods of ownership structures used today.

Chapter Four: Group Ownership Entities You May Use

Once the determination has been made that the potential investors in your next group do not require tax deferral through an IRC Section 1031 exchange and will not require the establishment of a tenant-in-common ownership structure, you will have to determine which legal entity you will use to gather your investors together and take title to the property.

Corporations

An association of two or more persons acting as co-owners of a business for profit may conduct their business in such a way as to be considered a corporation. A corporation is an entity formed under state laws. Corporations issue shares of stock to investors who become shareholders. The shareholders elect the Board of Directors who oversee the operations and hire the officers and managers to provide daily management of the business of the corporation. Corporations are generally referred to as C Corporations or *full-blown* corporations.

The corporation is generally formed upon the filing of Articles of Incorporation with the Secretary of State. Bylaws are drafted and become the rules for the conduct of business by the corporation.

Corporate characteristics

Corporations have each of the following characteristics:
- Limited liability of shareholders
- Free transferability of shares
- Continuity of life
- Separation of management from ownership

When looking at an enterprise to determine how it will be treated by the IRS, the first level of review will be to determine the presence of corporate characteristics. If the enterprise exhibits all of the four corporate characteristics listed, it will be treated by the law as a corporation.

Advantages of corporate ownership entity

Advantages of operating in a corporate entity would include:

- Limited liability for shareholders
- Governance structure that allows for management to be separate from ownership
- Consistency of law regarding the governance and securities treatment of corporations
- Possibility of anonymity of the owner of the shares
- Advantages to shareholder-employees in areas of benefits and retirement accounts
- Free transferability of ownership interests
- Flexibility in the ability to capitalize the entity
- Familiarity of the public with the corporate entity

The corporation is the favored choice of entity for most operating business ventures. The flexibility in capitalization and the free transferability of the shares allow the corporate entity to avail itself to the public marketplace and raise unlimited amounts of capital from an unlimited number of investors.

Disadvantages of corporate ownership entity

Disadvantages of operating in a corporate entity would include:

- Double taxation
- Substantial regulations and requirements of formal operating procedures
- Taxability of dispositions and liquidations

The corporate entity provides for taxation at the corporate level and at the shareholder level. For example, if the corporation reports annual income, the corporation must pay taxes at the appropriate corporate rates. In addition, when the corporation distributes dividends to the shareholders, the shareholders are subject to taxation on the reportable amount of dividends at their marginal tax rate.

As a security measure for the shareholders, the corporation and its officers and directors are subject to regulation and reporting requirements that are quite burdensome. In addition, corporate formalities require regularly scheduled meetings of shareholders, mandatory filing of reports with government agencies, and the keeping of corporate minutes including corporate resolutions.

Using corporations for group investment in real estate

It is unlikely the corporate entity will be the choice a sponsor would make for the entity in which their group would own investment real estate. Along with the burdensome formalities, the major disadvantages would be the double taxation of earnings and the lack of the ability to pass-through losses to the shareholders.

The double taxation would impact the annual earnings of your real estate, and the corporation will pay taxes on the annual real estate taxable income reported on the operations of the property. If the corporation is able to distribute positive cash flow to the shareholders in the form of dividends, the shareholders must also pay taxes.

For example, if the corporation reports $100,000 of taxable income on the operations of a property and is in a 34% tax bracket, the corporation will pay $34,000 in taxes. Assuming the taxable income is also the cash available for distribution, there will be $64,000 remaining that is available to distribute to the shareholders. If the shareholders are all in the 35% tax bracket and the $64,000 of dividends are reportable, another $22,400 would be paid in taxes. The result is the $100,000 of cash flow will be reduced by the payment of taxes at two levels in the total of $56,400, leaving $43,600 to be spent. The double taxation results in a combined 56.4% tax rate and will likely be higher with the inclusion of the calculation of state income taxes at both the corporate and shareholder level.

If the corporation reports $100,000 of taxable loss on the operations of a property, the losses stay at the corporate level and are not passed through to the shareholders so they could report the results on their individual tax returns.

S Corporations

The term S corporation refers to an elective status given to a corporation by federal and state law, allowing it to retain its corporate characteristics while avoiding double taxation by allowing the direct pass-through of taxable income or losses to the shareholders. Under certain circumstances, C corporations may elect to be converted to S corporations after formation.

S corporations must comply with certain restrictions not applied to C corporations. The number of shareholders is limited to seventy-five. They must all be individuals (or certain trusts and estates) and must be US residents. No artificial entities are allowed to invest in an S corporation. There can only be one class of stock issued. S corporations, while classified as securities, can be offered in private offerings.

While the S corporation eliminates double taxation and allows for the pass- through of losses to the individual shareholders, eliminating the two major disadvantages of using the corporate entity for group ownership of investment real estate, one significant disadvantage remains. *S corporations may not receive more than 20% of their annual income in the form of* passive *income, and under the S corporation rules, real estate rental income is defined as* passive income.

It is unlikely that an investment group formed to own income-producing real estate would choose an S corporation as the ownership entity. An S corporation could be used if the activity of the group is as a *dealer*, such as construction or land assemblage with subsequent individual parcel sales or development but little rental income. Also, some groups of individuals who want to be in the business as group sponsors choose to incorporate and select the status of an S corporation. That is the entity I used when I was an active syndicator, but if I were choosing today, I would likely choose a limited liability company.

Uniform Partnership Act

If an association of people is formed to carry on a business for profit but does not have the characteristics of a corporation, the entity may well be classified as a partnership. In this chapter, there will be a discussion of several types of associations that could be used for the group ownership of investment real estate that are not corporations and may be treated as partnerships. The classification of these entities as partnerships has its foundation in the Uniform Partnership Act (UPA). The UPA was originally passed in 1914. The UPA is administered by the National Conference of Commissioners on Uniform State Laws www.nccusl.org.

The UPA has been adopted in every state other than Louisiana. The UPA governs general partnerships and limited partnerships except when there is a written partnership agreement that is in accord with a specific state's enacted partnership laws. The UPA was modified in 1994 and renamed the Revised Uniform Partnership Act (RUPA) and was further modified in 1997 to include provisions for limited liability partnerships. The new provisions have been adopted, in part, in twenty-five states.

Specific state partnership laws would take precedence over the RUPA, but the RUPA acts almost as a state law in states where no partnership law exists or in matters where a partnership agreement is not formalized or silent on specific issues. The primary focus of RUPA is the small, often informal, partnership. Larger, more formal partnerships generally have a more formal partnership agreement addressing, and often modifying, many of the provisions of the RUPA.

Here are some of the general provisions of the RUPA that a sponsor of group investments must be aware of when setting up an entity to own investment real estate.

Definition of partnership

RUPA defines a partnership as:

> **the association of two or more persons to carry on as co-owners a business for profit forms a partnership, whether or not the persons intend to form a partnership. Section 202 (a)**

The two major elements of the definition are that there is an *association* of two or more persons and that they are operating a *business for profit*. That is a very broad statement that potentially would include every ownership situation where there will be more than one investor in an ownership position driven to produce a profit. But, not every instance of joint ownership or sharing of cash flows is considered a partnership.

The RUPA states that a joint tenancy, tenancy in common, tenancy by the entireties, joint property, community property, or part ownership does not by itself establish a partnership, even if the co-owners share profits made by the use of the property. Also, the sharing of gross returns does not by itself establish a partnership, even if the persons sharing them have a joint or common right or interest in property from which the returns are derived.

The group sponsor will likely be involved with a group in a way that will likely be classified as a partnership. This will not cause trouble unless the sponsor is attempting to operate in a tenant-in-common method, as discussed in the previous chapter.

Determination of who is a partner

RUPA states that a

> **person who receives a share of the profits of a business is presumed to be a partner in the business unless the profits were received in payment:**
> - **of a debt by installments or otherwise;**
> - **for services as an independent contractor or of wages or other compensation to an employee;**
> - **of rent;**
> - **of an annuity or other retirement or health benefit to a beneficiary, representative, or designee of a deceased or retired partner;**

- of interest or other charge on a loan, even if the amount of payment varies with the profits of the business, including a direct or indirect present or future ownership of the collateral, or rights to income, proceeds, or increase in value derived from the collateral; or
- for the sale of the goodwill of a business or other property by installments or otherwise. Section 202 (c)(3)

The sponsor must use care to be sure that people who wish to do business with the investment group they are forming will not be treated as partners if they are not intended to be partners.

Partnership property

The RUPA states that

> **Property acquired by a partnership is property of the partnership and not of the partners individually. Section 203**

This statement stands for the assumption that when a partner invests in a partnership to own investment real estate, what the partner receives is not an ownership interest in the property but an ownership interest in the partnership. The results of this distinction will be discussed in the chapter covering the classification of assets.

Partners have agency duty Section 301

The RUPA states that

> **Each partner is an agent of the partnership for the purpose of its business. An act of a partner, including the execution of an instrument in the partnership name, for apparently carrying on in the ordinary course the partnership business or business of the kind carried on by the partnership binds the partnership, unless the partner had no authority to act for the partnership in the particular matter and the person with whom the partner was dealing knew or had received a notification the partner lacked authority.**

The agency relationship and the resulting duties, including the potential for the existence of a fiduciary duty, were discussed in Chapter One.

Partnership is liable for acts of the partners

A partnership is liable for

> **loss or injury caused to a person, or for a penalty incurred as a result of a wrongful act or omission, or other actionable conduct of a partner, acting in the ordinary course of business of the partnership or with authority of the partnership. Section 305**

Investors in a partnership, including any general partner of a general partnership or the general partner of a limited partnership may act inappropriately and, as a result, create liability for the partnership.

Partners are liable

The general rule is that

> **all partners are liable jointly and severally for all obligations of the partnership unless otherwise agreed to by the claimant or provided by law. Section 306**

This rule is modified in a limited partnership where the limited partners are prohibited from acting in the daily business of the partnership.

A person admitted as a partner into an existing partnership is not personally liable for any partnership obligation incurred before the person's admission as a partner.

Actions by and against the partnership and partners

The general rule is

> **a partnership may sue and be sued in the name of the partnership. Section 307**

In general, an action may be brought against the partnership, and any or all of the partners in the same action or in separate actions.

A judgment against a partnership is not by itself a judgment against a partner. A judgment against a partnership may not be satisfied from a partner's assets unless a judgment creditor obtains a separate judgment against the partner.

A judgment creditor who obtains a judgment against a partner, based on a judgment awarded against the partnership, may not levy execution against the personal assets of the partner, unless the partner has been held to be personally liable for the claim; and a judgment based on the same claim has been obtained against the partnership and a writ of execution on the judgment has been returned unsatisfied in whole or in part; or

the partnership is a debtor in bankruptcy; or

the partner has agreed the creditor need not exhaust partnership assets; or

liability is imposed on the partner by law or contract independent of the existence of the partnership.

A partner is not co-owner of partnership property

In general,

> **a partner is not a co-owner of the partnership property and has no interest in partnership property which can be transferred, either voluntarily or involuntarily. Section 501**

This distinction is important in the event of the death, bankruptcy, divorce, or other claim against the assets of a partner. The person or court bringing the claim cannot look to the property owned by the partnership for repayment, but may only look to the partnership interests. This is different than the treatment in a tenant-in-common relationship where, to satisfy certain claims, the court may order the partition of the property, which will likely result in the forced sale of the entire property to satisfy the claim.

General Partnerships

When a small group of investors get together to pool resources and each investor wants to participate in the daily management decisions, a general partnership may be the correct legal entity to choose.

A joint venture or strategic partnership is a business relationship created by contract between two or more individuals or business entities who wish to jointly engage in a specific activity for a limited period of time. Investment groups operating as joint ventures are going to be treated as general partnerships. A construction company may join up with an insurance company to develop an office building. Neither the construction company nor the insurance company would be in a position to complete the project on their own as the construction company likely lacks adequate equity and the insurance company likely lacks the construction expertise needed to complete the project.

Two or more people

A general partnership can be formed by as few as two people or entities with each being a general partner. The key document needed for the operation of a general partnership is the General Partnership Agreement.

Who can be a member?

In general partnerships, there are few restrictions as to who can be a partner. In limited partnerships and corporations, specifically S corporations, there are restrictions as to who can be a partner or a shareholder. Check with your attorney to see if a foreign investor or corporation can be a general partner in your state. Other than the requirement of a minimum of two partners, there are no restrictions as to the number of partners in a general partnership.

All general partners share equally in management

As a general partner, each person or entity has the ability to participate in the daily management of the property owned by the general partnership. This characteristic of a general partnership is ideal for a small group of investors who each have a particular expertise. However, this characteristic makes it impractical for a large number of investors in that management decisions become more difficult with larger numbers of equal decision makers.

Joint and several liability

Each general partner has personal liability for the actions of the partnership. Each general partner is totally liable for all the debts of the partnership regardless of the amount of money each partner invests in the general partnership. This is one of the major drawbacks of using a general partnership entity to own investment real estate.

For example, assume that in a general partnership, one general partner invests $500,000 in cash and the other general partner invests $10 million in cash. Collectively, the two individual general partners are totally liable for the debts of the general partnership. In addition, regardless of what role each general partner agrees to take in the management of the business of the partnership, each general partner is individually liable for the total liabilities of the property owned by the partnership.

Fiduciary duty

Each partner in a general partnership has a fiduciary duty to the other partners. Fiduciary duty exists whenever one person, the client, places special trust and confidence in another person and relies upon that person to exercise his discretion or expertise in acting for the client. The fiduciary knowingly accepts that trust and confidence and, as a result, undertakes to act on behalf of the client by exercising discretion and expertise.

A person who is owed a fiduciary duty has a right to expect the fiduciary will:
- Use his best efforts when acting on their behalf
- Not act in any manner adverse or contrary to their interests
- Not act on his own behalf in relation to their interests
- Exercise all of the skill, care and due diligence at his disposal

In addition, a person acting as a fiduciary is required to make truthful and complete disclosures so that informed decisions may be made and the fiduciary is forbidden to obtain an unreasonable advantage at the expense of the client.

Duty of care
General partners are required to perform their duties with the care, skill, diligence, and prudence of like persons in like positions.

Each general partner will be required to make decisions employing the diligence, care, and skill an ordinary prudent person would exercise in the management of their own affairs. This is known as the prudent investor rule which is applied to the actions of the general partner to determine if the general partner performed their fiduciary duties in an appropriate manner.

The *business judgment rule* is the standard applied when determining what constitutes care, skill, diligence, and prudence of like persons in like positions. This rule does not include the examination of the substantive merits of business decisions made by group managers that own investment real estate, but looks at
potential conflicts of interests which were intentionally hidden; or
failure to follow reasonable procedures, such as failure to obtain professional appraisals before selling a property; or
failure to consider potential competing offers from potential buyers or potential tenants.

Duty of disclosure
Each general partner has an affirmative duty to disclose material facts to all other general partners. It is unlawful for general partners to make untrue statements regarding material facts or to omit telling the other general partners about a material fact.

Duty of loyalty

General partners have a duty to avoid conflicts of interests. Before raising money from investors, the general partner must disclose any conflict of interest that may exist with the interests of the partnership or the other general partners.

General partners are restricted from entering into contracts with the partnership that favor the business interests of the general partner over the business interests of the partnership.

General partners may not profit from opportunities presented to them that are related to the business of the partnership and are not offered to the partnership first, regardless of whether the partnership has the funds needed to act on the opportunity.

Title to the property is held in the name of the partnership

In a general partnership, the title to the property is held by the general partnership, not in the names of the individual general partners. For example, A&B partnership is made up of two general partners, A and B. The title to the property may read "A&B, a General Partnership." The general partnership owns the real estate. Each of the individual general partners owns a personal property interest in the partnership.

Advantage of ownership of personal property interest

The distinction as to who owns what is important in certain situations, such as the death, divorce, or bankruptcy of one of the general partners. Since what is owned by the general partner is simply an ownership interest in an entity, that ownership interest may be transferred without requiring the sale of the real estate. The feature of the ownership interest being transferable without the sale of the real estate is an advantage a general partnership entity has over that of a tenant-in-common ownership of the property.

In certain events, such as death, divorce, or bankruptcy of one of the individual owners, it is possible the only way to solve the problems created by such an event would be to sell the property to generate cash. In certain situations, the courts may direct an asset to be sold to provide the solution that is needed. The forced sale of an asset may put one or more of the other owners in an unfavorable situation, such as not being able to structure the sale so as to accommodate the 45-day and 180-day rules in an IRC Section 1031 tax deferred exchange. If the asset was a personal property interest, it is likely the real estate would not have to be sold to provide the needed solution.

Disadvantage of ownership of personal property interest

A disadvantage to the ownership of a personal property interest is that, while the ownership interest is transferable, it may not have the same value as a corresponding direct ownership interest in the real estate owned by the general partnership. The lack of the ability of a holder of the interest to convert their ownership interest into cash, at full market value, is a disadvantage of ownership by an entity such as a general partnership.

With regards to IRC Section 1031 tax deferred exchanges, it is generally the rule that, as the general partnership owns real the estate, the general partnership may take advantage of tax deferral available in an exchange of real estate. The general partners, do not have direct ownership of real estate, and have a very limited ability to exchange their partnership interests for other partnership interests and defer the recognition of gain on the exchange.

Partnership is a tax-reporting entity; partners pay taxes

At the end of the taxable year, the general partnership will arrange for a CPA to prepare and file a Federal Income Tax Return on Form 1065. This document is an informational return that reports the results of the operation of the business of the general partnership for the year. No tax is paid by the general partnership as a general partnership is a pass-through entity in that all the taxable results are reported on the tax returns of the individual general partners, not the general partnership.

The general partnership will prepare and distribute a Schedule K-1 to each of the individual general partners. The Schedule K-1 will be used by each general partner to report their portion of the taxable income or loss from the operations of the property for the tax year on the appropriate Section of their IRS Form 1040.

One advantage in using a general partnership as a legal entity to own investment real estate is that it is a pass-through entity. As such, there is no tax paid at the entity level, and taxable income or loss flows directly to the individual who may be able to use the income or losses to offset other income or loss he may have.

Special allocations

In a general partnership, there may be the possibility of providing disproportionate allocations of cash distributions and taxable income or losses among general partners. An example would be to allocate a disproportionate share of cash flow to one general partner and a disproportionate share of taxable income to another general partner. This is an area of complexity that must be addressed by a tax attorney or CPA to assure the allocations have a business purpose and are not designed for tax avoidance.

Multiple classes are not allowed
Generally, there is only one class of partner present in a general partnership.

Corporate characteristics must not be present in a general partnership
Generally, a corporation has each of the following characteristics:
- Limited liability of shareholders
- Free transferability of shares
- Continuity of life
- Separation of management from ownership

Historically, at the federal level and currently in many states, a general partnership wishing to avoid being treated as a corporation for tax purposes and to retain the status of a pass-through entity must not have more than two of the above listed corporate formalities.

The two corporate characteristics that a general partnership can avoid are the characteristics of continuity of life and free transferability. To overcome the unlimited life characteristic, a general partnership agreement will state a finite term, such as five or ten years. The general partnership agreement will also include a clause that places restrictions on the ability of the partners to transfer their interests, thereby overcoming the characteristic of free transferability.

"Check-the-box" method of classifying an entity for tax purposes
In **Treasury Decision 8697, published in the Federal Register for December 18, 1996,** the IRS adopted regulations simplifying the *classification of entity* issue in investment groups. As applied on the federal level, these regulations replace the four-prong test that has historically been applied to determine the classification of the entity.

Partnership tax treatment is the default method for investment groups
The recent adoption by the IRS of the "check-the-box" regulations establishes a partnership as the federal tax default classification for general partnerships. No action is needed to be taken by the general partnership that wants to be taxed as a partnership. The most important issue here is these regulations make the analysis of the corporate characteristic a moot issue for partnerships formed after January 1, 1997.

State laws may differ

However, not all states have adopted the "check-the-box" approach, and it is still advisable to discuss with your attorney or CPA the issue of including a restriction on the transferability of interests and inserting a definite term of life for the entity upon its organization.

Limited Partnership

When a large number of investors need to pool their resources and, as a result, management authority must be concentrated in one or a small number of persons, a limited partnership may be the best ownership entity to use. The investors do not want to take part in the daily management of the limited partnership and, as a result, agree to give management authority to one or a small number of people.

The key document needed for the operation of a limited partnership is the Limited Partnership Agreement.

Advantages of a limited partnership

Generally, the advantages of the limited partnership as an entity would be listed as:

- Pass through tax treatment
- No dissolution on the withdrawal of a limited partner
- Less regulation and formalities than a corporation
- Flexibility in allocating income and losses
- A well-developed body of law governing limited partnerships
- No taxable event on liquidation

Disadvantages of a limited partnership

Generally, the disadvantages of the limited partnership as an entity would be listed as:

- Unlimited liability of the general partner(s)
- Inability of the limited partners to actively participate in management
- Partner consent is required for continuation of limited partnership after the death or withdrawal of a general partner
- Requirement there be two or more partners
- Requirement the limited partnership provide limited partners with annual information tax returns
- Unsuitability of using a limited partnership as a vehicle for a public offering
- Classification of limited partnership interests as investment contracts and, as a result, a possible treatment as a security

Two or more partners

A limited partnership must have two or more partners. One partner must be willing to act as a general partner to manage the partnership and assume the position of having the authority to bind the partnership. The general partner will have unlimited liability for all the debts of the partnership. The remaining partners would be classified as limited partners. Limited partners are allowed no part in the daily management decisions of the limited partnership and have limited liability for the debts of the limited partnership.

Who can be a member?

In limited partnerships, there are some restrictions as to who can be a partner. Check with your attorney to see if a foreign investor or corporation can be a limited partner in your limited partnership. Other than the requirement of a minimum of two partners, there are no restrictions as to the number of partners in a limited partnership.

General partner performs all management functions

By definition, a limited partner has limited involvement in the daily management of the partnership and no involvement in the daily management of the property, leaving all of the management authority to the general partner. In order to protect the status of having limited liability by virtue of being considered a limited partner, the partner must not take any actions that would cause the partner to be reclassified as a general partner, which would put the partner in the position of having unlimited liability.

Theory of fiduciary duty

It is well established that the general partner or partners owe a fiduciary duty to the limited partners.

Fiduciary contract

A fiduciary contract exists when one person delivers a thing—such as trust, confidence, or money—to another person on the condition the thing will be returned at some future time. During the time the fiduciary is in possession of the thing belonging to the other person, the fiduciary must act in the best interests of the person to whom the thing must be returned.

When an investor invests in a limited partnership a contract is formed between the partner and the general partner of the limited partnership. A fiduciary relationship is established as a result of the limited partner delivering money to the general partner. A general partner has a fiduciary duty to the investors in the limited partnership. As long as the general partner is in possession of the partners' money, the general partner must act in the best interests of the limited partners.

Fiduciary duty

Each partner in a general partnership has a fiduciary duty to each other partner. As described in Chapter One, fiduciary duty exists whenever one person, the client, places special trust and confidence in another person and relies upon that person to exercise his discretion or expertise in acting for the client. The fiduciary knowingly accepts that trust and confidence and, as a result, undertakes to act on behalf of the client by exercising discretion and expertise.

Persons who are owed a fiduciary duty have a right to expect the fiduciary will
   use their best efforts when acting on their behalf;
   not act in any manner adverse or contrary to their interests;
   not act on their own behalf in relation to their interests; and
   exercise all of the skill, care and due diligence at their disposal.

In addition, a person acting as a fiduciary is required to make truthful and complete disclosures so that informed decisions may be made. The fiduciary is forbidden to obtain an unreasonable advantage at the expense of the client.

Duty of care

Just as officers and directors of corporations owe a fiduciary duty to their shareholders, general partners of limited partnerships are required to perform their duties with the care, skill, diligence, and prudence of like persons in like positions.

The general partner will be required to make decisions employing the diligence, care, and skill an ordinary prudent person would exercise in the management of his own affairs. This is known as the prudent investor rule and is applied to the actions of the general partner to determine if the general partner performed their fiduciary duties in an appropriate manner.

The business judgment rule is the standard applied when determining what constitutes care, skill, diligence, and prudence of like persons in like positions. This rule does not include the examination of the substantive merits of business decisions made by group managers that own investment real estate, but looks at
   potential conflicts of interest which were intentionally hidden; or
   failure to follow reasonable procedures such as failure to obtain professional appraisals before selling a property; or

failure to consider potential competing offers from potential buyers or potential tenants.

General partners are required to make well-informed, independent, good faith decisions on behalf of the investment group.

Duty of disclosure

General partners of limited partnerships have an affirmative duty to disclose material facts to the limited partners. It is unlawful for general partners to make untrue statements regarding material facts or to omit telling the limited partners about a material fact.

Information is considered material if there is a substantial likelihood that a reasonable investor would consider it important in making an investment decision.

When the limited partners are in a position to vote for a major event, the general partner must disclose to them the material information needed for them to give an informed consent to the suggested action.

Duty of loyalty

General partners have a duty to avoid conflicts of interest. Before raising money from limited partners, the general partner must disclose any conflict of interest that may exist with the interests of the limited partnership or the individual limited partners.

General partners are restricted from entering into contracts with a limited partnership that favors the business interests of the general partner over the business interests of the limited partnership.

General partners may not profit from opportunities that are related to the business of the limited partnership and are not offered to the limited partnership first, regardless of whether the limited partnership has the funds needed to act on the opportunity.

Limited partners do not have a fiduciary duty

Just as it is well established that the general partner has a fiduciary duty to the limited partners, it is well established the limited partners have no fiduciary duty to each other.

The limited partnership agreement states the role of a limited partner is as a passive investor and, as such, the limited partner takes no part in the daily management of the partnership. As the limited partner has a passive role, there is no fiduciary contract created among the limited partners with each other. Lacking a fiduciary contract between limited partners, there can be no fiduciary duty owed between limited partners.

Limited partners have limited liability

Limited partners are only liable for the money they have at risk. Assume that a limited partner has invested $50,000 cash. That is all the money the limited partner could lose in the investment. His liability is limited to the amount of money he has *at risk*.

Some limited partnerships have provisions for additional investments over and above the original investment. This provision is sometimes called a *capital call* or an *assessment provision*. A capital call or assessment provision would be common in a limited partnership document when the property is a development project. The total initial investment may have been $1 million, but a clause is contained in the partnership document requiring the limited partners to contribute $5 million of additional cash upon the start of construction. If a provision such as this is found in the partnership agreement, the limited partner would also be liable for their portion of the subsequent investment. Even with a capital call or assessment provision, the limited partner knows at the outset the total extent of their liability or the total amount they have at risk.

In order to maintain the limited liability feature, each limited partner must limit their involvement in daily management of the limited partnership. Limited partners must be *passive* with regards to management of the partnership's business. If an investor begins to take part in management, the investor suddenly looks like a general partner to the IRS and faces the potential of losing their protection of limited liability.

Title to the property is held in the name of the partnership

In a limited partnership, the title to the property is held by the limited partnership, not in the names of the individual partners. For example, A&B Limited Partnership is made up of two general partners, A and B and eight limited partners. The title to the property may read "A&B, a Limited Partnership." The limited partnership owns the real estate. Each of the individual general partners and limited partners owns a personal property interest in the partnership.

Partnership interests are illiquid

The ownership interests in a limited partnership are personal property, not real property. There is seldom a market for the sale of a limited partnership interest. An investor in a limited partnership must be prepared to stay in the partnership until the property investment cycle is completed.

Partnership is a tax reporting entity; partners pay taxes

During the first quarter of the year, the general partner will cause the limited partnership to file an informational Form 1065 return with the IRS reporting the results of the operations of the limited partnership for the prior year. The general partner will then distribute a Schedule K-1 to each limited partner, who then reports his share of income or expense on his own tax return.

One advantage in using a limited partnership as a legal entity to own investment real estate is that it is a pass-through entity. As such, taxable income or losses flow directly to the individual who may be able to use the income or losses to offset other income or losses he may have.

Passive activity

Limited partnership interests are by definition passive activities and, as such, are affected by the restrictions in the current IRC passive loss rules.

This is a very complicated area of the tax law, in that a limited partnership interest is a passive activity, and limited partners may accumulate suspended losses which may be used on the disposition of the partnership interest to offset any passive income. However, it is possible the general partner of the limited partnership could be determined to be active, depending upon their level of involvement in the management of the property.

Special allocations

In a limited partnership there is the possibility of providing disproportionate allocations of cash distributions and taxable income or losses among limited partners. An example would be to allocate a disproportionate share of cash flow to one limited partner and a disproportionate share of taxable income to another limited partner. This is an area of complexity that must be addressed by a tax attorney or CPA to assure the allocations have a business purpose and are not designed for tax avoidance.

Multiple classes allowed

In a limited partnership, there could be multiple classes of investors. One class of investors could be lenders; another class could be equity investors who want a preferred return; and another class could be equity investors who want the tax shelter and appreciation.

For example, there can be what is called an "AB Partnership." The owners of the A units are typically tax exempt investors, such as a self-directed IRAs, and are to be paid a preferred return that constitutes most of the distributable cash flow. The owners of the B units are typically taxpayers and are to receive the balance of the cash flows, if any, the appreciation of the property, and the cost recovery deductions.

This is also an area of complexity that must be addressed by a tax attorney or CPA to assure the multiple classifications of units serve a business purpose and are not designed for tax avoidance.

Corporate formalities must not be present in a limited partnership

Generally, a corporation has each of the following characteristics:
- Limited liability of shareholders
- Free transferability of shares
- Continuity of life
- Separation of management from ownership

Historically, at the federal level and currently in many states, a limited partnership wanting to avoid being treated as a corporation for tax purposes and to retain the status of a pass-through entity, must not have more than two of the above listed corporate formalities. Two of the corporate characteristics are likely to be present in a limited partnership. The two corporate characteristics that a limited partnership can avoid are the characteristics of continuity of life and free transferability. To overcome the unlimited life characteristic, a limited partnership agreement will state a finite term, such as five or ten years. The limited partnership agreement will also include a clause that places restrictions on the ability of the partners to transfer their interests, thereby overcoming the characteristic of free transferability.

"Check-the-box" method of classifying an entity for tax purposes

In **Treasury Decision 8697, published in the Federal Register for December 18, 1996**, the IRS adopted regulations simplifying the *classification of entity* issue in investment groups. As applied on the federal level, these regulations replace the four-prong test which has historically been applied to determine the classification of the entity.

Partnership tax treatment is the default method for investment groups

The recent adoption by the IRS of the so-called "check-the-box" regulations sets partnership as the federal tax default classification for limited partnerships being formed today. No action is needed to be taken by the limited partnership. The most important issue here is these regulations make the analysis of the corporate characteristic a moot issue for partnerships formed after January 1, 1997.

State taxation may be different

However, not all states have adopted the "check-the-box" approach and it is still advisable to discuss with your attorney or CPA the issue of including a restriction on the transferability of interests and inserting a definite term of life for the entity upon its organization.

> *TIP: One of the most attractive features of general or limited partnerships is the pass-through of losses or income to the partners without any payment of taxes at the partnership level. Because the partnership only reports income or loss and does not pay taxes, taxes are only paid once in a partnership as opposed to a corporation which pays taxes as well as the shareholders, which is double taxation. Limited partnerships offer the additional advantage of providing the limited partner with limited liability as opposed to the unlimited liability found in a general partnership.*

Limited Liability Company (LLC)

The first limited liability company law was passed in Wyoming in 1977. In 1988, the IRS formally approved this structure and, today, all fifty states have approved legislation to enable the formation and operation of limited liability companies. In many states, a limited liability company may be formed with only one member. A limited liability company is owned by the members who manage the entity directly or appoint managers to operate the entity and supervise the managers hired to run the daily activities of the entity.

Reasons for the establishment of limited liability companies

In the 1980s, the syndication industry was experiencing difficult times because of the loss in value of energy and real estate partnerships. The ability to raise capital for new ventures was limited because of two main reasons:

- The unwillingness of group sponsors to take on the unlimited liability which came with being a general partner in a limited partnership
- The unwillingness of investors, who wanted to participate in the daily management of the properties in which they invested, to assume the unlimited liability that came with being a general partner

Limited liability company laws were written by individual states to address these issues by granting limited liability to all members, including the managing member, allowing group members to take an active role in management while still maintaining limited liability and providing a legal entity with less cumbersome operating requirements. The purpose of the limited liability company laws was to facilitate the formation of capital.

The key documents for a limited liability company are the Articles of Organization and the Operating Agreement.

A limited liability company created under the laws of one state may do business in other states by registering the limited liability company in each state in which it desires to do business.

Advantages of a limited liability company

Generally, the advantages of the limited liability company as an entity would be listed as:

- Pass-through tax treatment
- No dissolution on the withdrawal of a member
- Less regulation and formalities than a corporation
- Flexibility in allocating income and losses
- No taxable event on liquidation
- Possible treatment of a member's activity as material participation

Disadvantages of a limited liability company

Generally, the disadvantages of the limited liability company as an entity would be listed as:

- Uncertainty as to the body of law regarding limited liability companies
- Most states allow formation with only one investor
- The general requirement of the use of calendar year tax reporting
- Uncertainty of the application of securities laws to the interests in limited liability companies
- Possible treatment of the investor's activity as passive

One or more members

Your state's limited liability company law will specify the minimum number of people needed to form a limited liability company. Most allow single member limited liability companies.

Who can be a member?

There are fewer restrictions as to who can become a member of a limited liability company than other entities. In limited partnerships and corporations, specifically S corporations, there are restrictions as to who can be a partner or a shareholder. Many of these restrictions are eliminated in limited liability companies. For example many states have limited liability company laws that have no restrictions against foreign investors being a member of the group or any restrictions against a corporation being a member of a group.

Managing member's duties

The managing member will have responsibilities and management duties as outlined in the Operating Agreement.

Limited liability is available for all members of the group

In a limited liability company investors are called group members, not shareholders or partners. All group members can have limited liability, whether or not they are active or passive with regard to their role in management.

This is a major difference between limited partnerships and limited liability companies and allows the members of a limited liability company to take an active role in the management of the business of the group without losing the feature of limited liability. In addition, it is possible that a member of a limited liability company could be considered to be a material participant as that applies to the application of the passive loss rule.

Limited Liability Company is a tax reporting entity; members pay taxes

During the first quarter of the year, the managing member will cause the limited liability company to file an informational Form 1065 return with the IRS reporting the results of the operations of the limited liability company for the prior year. The managing member will then distribute a Schedule K-1 to each group member, who then reports their share of income or expense on their own tax return. A limited liability company is a pass-through entity in that there is no taxable income reported at the partnership level. As such, taxable income or losses flow directly to the individual members who may be able to use the income or losses to offset other income or losses they may have.

Pass-through entity

In a limited liability company, income or loss from the operation of the business is passed directly through to the members of the group without being taxed at the organization level.

To qualify for this pass-through characteristic, the limited liability company must have two characteristics in its legal agreement by which the entity is managed. First, ownership interests in the limited liability company may not be freely transferred, and secondly, the agreement must include a provision the limits the life of the limited liability company.

TIP: In a limited liability company, a member may be involved in the daily management of the business of the group. Also, the taxable income or taxable losses are passed through to the individual members. These two characteristics of limited liability companies have great significance in that it may be possible for a member of a limited liability company to qualify as a material participant in a rental activity and avoid the passive loss restrictions.

Special allocations

In a limited liability company, there is the possibility of providing disproportionate allocations of cash distributions and taxable income or losses among group members. An example would be to allocate a disproportionate share of cash flow to one member and a disproportionate share of taxable income to another member. This is an area of complexity that must be addressed by a tax attorney or CPA to assure the allocations have a business purpose and are not designed for tax avoidance.

Multiple classes allowed

In a limited liability company, there can be multiple classes of investors. One class of investors could be lenders, another class could be equity investors who want a preferred return, and another class could be equity investors who want the tax shelter and appreciation.

Corporate formalities must not be present in a limited liability company

Generally, a corporation has each of the following characteristics:

- limited liability of shareholders
- free transferability of shares
- continuity of life
- separation of management from ownership

Historically, at the federal level and currently in many states, a limited liability company wanting to avoid being treated as a corporation for tax purposes and retain the status of a pass-through entity must not have more than two of the above-listed corporate formalities. Two of the corporate characteristics are likely to be present in a limited liability company. To overcome the unlimited life characteristic, the operating agreement will state a finite term, such as five or ten years. The operating agreement will also include a clause that places restrictions on the ability of the partners to transfer their interests, thereby overcoming the characteristic of free transferability.

"Check-the-box" method of classifying an entity for tax purposes

In **Treasury Decision 8697, published in the Federal Register for December 18, 1996,** the IRS adopted regulations simplifying the *classification of entity* issue in investment groups. As applied on the federal level, these regulations replace the four-prong test which has historically been applied to determine the classification of the entity. However, not all states have adopted this approach and it is still advisable to discuss with your attorney or CPA the issue of including a restriction on the transferability of interests and inserting a definite term of life for the entity upon its organization.

Partnership tax treatment is the default method for investment groups

The recent adoption by the IRS of the so-called "check-the-box" regulations sets partnership as the federal tax default classification for limited liability companies being formed today. A limited liability company could elect to be taxed as a corporation by completing and filing IRS Form 8832 according to the regulations. No action is needed to be taken by the limited liability company if it does not elect to be taxed as a corporation. Any election to be made must be made during a time period starting no earlier than seventy-five days prior to the filing date of the company or no later than twelve months after the filing date.

This "check-the-box" approach is also available for limited liability companies that were in existence prior to January 1, 1977, the effective date of this regulation. An entity may change its election but not more frequently than every sixty months.

Single member limited liability company status
Individuals who have the ability to form a single-person limited liability company under their state law will be treated under the federal rules as a sole proprietorship unless they file IRS Form 8832 and elect a change in status so as to be taxed as a corporation.

Less corporate formalities are required to protect the limited liability of group members
In limited liability companies, lack of corporate formalities, by themselves, will not allow creditors to proceed directly against a group member, bypassing the protection of limited liability as in corporations.

Limited liability companies operating as a corporation do not have to adhere to the formalities of a corporation. In corporations, when the corporate formalities are not adhered to creditors are able to *pierce the corporate veil* of protection normally available to the shareholder. The limited liability available to a shareholder in a corporation may be lost if the corporation fails to hold regular meetings or keep an updated set of corporate books. Limited liability companies do not have to include the requirement of annual meetings for the group members.

Evolving theory of fiduciary duty
It should be clear that the managing member of a limited liability company owes a fiduciary duty to the members of the group in the same manner that a general partner owes a fiduciary duty to the limited partners in a limited partnership.

An evolving area of the law is the existence of a fiduciary duty *on the part of each member* of a limited liability company towards the other members of the company. This duty would most likely exist in a limited liability company that allows for the direct management of the entity by the members.

Some attorneys are now suggesting their wealthiest clients invest as limited partners, rather than as members of limited liability companies, so as to eliminate the possibility of being determined to have a fiduciary duty to other investors in the group.

Fiduciary contract

A fiduciary contract exists when one person delivers a thing, such as trust, confidence, or money, to another person on the condition the thing will be returned at some future time. This contract need not be in writing. During the time the fiduciary is in possession of the thing belonging to the other person, the fiduciary must act in the best interests of the person to whom the thing must be returned.

When an investor invests in a limited liability company managed by its members, it could be argued that a reciprocal fiduciary contract is formed between all the members of the group. A fiduciary contract is established as a result of the members placing their money and trust in the hands of each of the other members of the group. As each member has a role in managing the group investment, each member can be said to have a fiduciary duty to the other members in the group. As long as the members are in possession of the other members' money, each member must act in the best interests of all the members.

Fiduciary duty

In a limited liability company, it can be argued that a fiduciary duty exists whenever one member places special trust and confidence in another member, and relies upon that member to exercise their discretion or expertise in their action regarding the investment. The other member knowingly accepts that trust and confidence and, as a result, undertakes to act on behalf of the other member by exercising discretion and expertise.

A person who is owed a fiduciary duty has a right to expect the fiduciary will:
- Use their best efforts when acting on their behalf
- Not act in any manner adverse or contrary to their interests
- Not act on their own behalf in relation to their interests
- Exercise all of the skill, care, and due diligence at their disposal

In addition, a person acting as a fiduciary is required to make truthful and complete disclosures so that informed decisions may be made, and the fiduciary is forbidden to obtain an unreasonable advantage at the expense of the client.

Duty of care

Just as officers and directors of corporations owe a fiduciary to their shareholders, group sponsors have a fiduciary duty to the investors in their groups. Group members who participate in the direct management of a limited liability company are required to perform their duties with the care, skill, diligence, and prudence of like persons in like positions.

The group members should be required to make decisions employing the diligence, care, and skill an ordinary prudent person would exercise in the management of his own affairs. This is known as the prudent investor rule which should be applied to the actions of the group member so as to determine if the group member performed their fiduciary duties in an appropriate manner.

The business judgment rule is the standard applied when determining what constitutes care, skill, diligence, and prudence of like persons in like positions. This rule does not include the examination of the substantive merits of business decisions of group members in limited liability companies that own investment real estate but looks at

> potential conflicts of interests which were intentionally hidden; or
> failure to follow reasonable procedures such as failure to obtain professional appraisals before selling a property; or
> failure to consider potential competing offers from potential buyers or potential tenants.

Group members are required to make well-informed, independent, good faith decisions on behalf of the investment group.

Duty of disclosure
Managing members of a limited liability company have an affirmative duty to disclose material facts to the members of the group. It is unlawful for managing members to make an untrue statement regarding a material fact or to omit to tell the group members of a material fact.

Information is considered material if there is a substantial likelihood that a reasonable investor would consider it important in making an investment decision.

When members of a limited liability company are in a position to vote for a major event, the managing member must disclose to the members the material information needed for them to give an informed consent to the suggested action.

Duty of loyalty

Managing members of limited liability companies have a duty to avoid conflicts of interests. Before raising money from investors, the managing member must disclose any conflict of interest that may exist with the interests of the limited liability company or the individual members.

Managing members are restricted from entering into contracts with a limited liability company that favors the business interests of the managing members over the business interests of the limited liability company.

Managing members of a limited liability company may not profit from opportunities presented to them related to the business of the limited liability company, and are not offered to the limited liability company first, regardless of whether the limited liability company has the funds needed to act on the opportunity.

Miscellaneous

It is possible that groups such as limited partnerships, general partnerships, and sole proprietors who wish to convert their current entity structure to a limited liability company may be able to contribute their property to a limited liability company on a tax-free basis. However, corporate conversion to a limited liability company is most likely a taxable event.

TIP: In a real estate venture, as well as any other business venture, it is seldom that one of the investors is willing to assume general liability for the entire obligations of the business as is required of the general partner in either a general partnership or limited partnership. The limited liability company is seen by many as offering the best protection from liability for the operation of the real estate business of these three pass-through entities.

Summary

In this chapter you learned about corporations, limited partnerships, and limited liability companies. Which one will you choose to conduct your next group investment? Making the entity decision is something you are not used to doing, but "It's a Whole New Business!"

In the next chapter, we will discuss securities laws and how they will apply to you. This is new information for many of you as group sponsors, and it is important to understand the securities laws because "It's a Whole New Business!"

Chapter Five: Securities Laws You Need to Know

The Securities Acts of 1933(as Amended 2012) and 1934 (as Amended 2012)

Purpose of the laws

Because of the amount of money lost in the financial industry crash of 1929, the federal government felt it needed legislation to protect investors. The federal legislation enacted in 1933 and 1934 is the basis for the security laws group sponsors work with today.

The Securities Acts of 1933 and 1934 were designed to protect the public from fraudulent investment securities and those who would sell fraudulent securities. They have two basic objectives:

- To require that investors receive financial and other significant information concerning securities being offered for sale to the public to allow for informed decisions (Securities Act of 1933)
- To prohibit deceit, misrepresentations, and other fraud in the sale of securities. (Securities Exchange Act of 1934)

The full text of The Securities Act of 1933 (as Amended in 2012) can be found at http://www.sec.gov/about/laws/sa33.pdf.

The full text of the Securities Exchange Act of 1934 (as Amended in 2012) can be found at http://www.sec.gov/about/laws/sea34.pdf.

Full disclosure is needed for informed decisions

A primary means of accomplishing the goal of having investors make informed decisions is requiring the full disclosure of important financial information throughout the process of the registration of the securities. While the government makes no judgment as to the merits of the security being registered, it is expected that the information required to be included in a registration statement will enable investors to make informed judgments about the units offered in the investment group. Investors who purchase securities and suffer losses have important recovery rights if they can prove there was incomplete or inaccurate disclosure of important information.

U.S. Securities and Exchange Commission (SEC)

The U.S. Securities and Exchange Commission (SEC) was created through the Securities Exchange Act of 1934. The Act empowers the SEC with broad authority over all aspects of the securities industry and charges the SEC with the administration of the securities laws and the registration process. The SEC requires that information provided in registration statements provided to potential investors is accurate. However, the SEC does not guarantee the accuracy of the disclosures. Because of the limited resources of the SEC, it is impossible for it to police every security offered in the United States and exemptions to the federal securities laws and the exemptions that have been enacted. Information about the SEC can be found at www.sec.gov.

What is a Security?

The word *security* is defined in **Section 2(1) of the Securities Act of 1933** as:

> **The term "security" means any note, stock, treasury stock, bond, debenture, evidence of indebtedness, certificate of interest or participation in any profit-sharing agreement, collateral-trust certificate, pre-organization certificate or subscription, transferable share, *investment contract* (emphasis added), voting trust certificate, certificate of deposit for a security, fractional undivided interest in oil, gas, or other mineral rights, any put, call, straddle, option, or privilege on any security, certificate of deposit, or group or index of securities (including any interest therein or based on the value thereof), or any put, call, straddle, option, or privilege entered into on a national securities exchange relating to foreign currency, or, in general, any interest or instrument commonly known as a "security," or any certificate of interest or participation in, temporary or interim certificate for, receipt for, guarantee of, or warrant or right to subscribe to or purchase any of the foregoing.**

While the list of investment vehicles that are defined as securities is quite lengthy, the Supreme Court, in **Reves v Ernst & Young, 494 U.S. 56, 61 (1990)**, expands the definition by stating the purpose of Congress in enacting the securities laws was to regulate investments in "whatever form they are made and by whatever name they are called." It appears the Supreme Court was saying the definition of security is intended to be broad enough to encompass almost any instrument that might be sold as an investment to a passive investor.

As it relates to commercial and investment real estate, it might not be an overstatement to say the intention of Congress was to consider any purchase of real estate that does not involve the direct purchase of a deeded interest in an entire property by one individual buyer *an investment contract*, and, as such, a security that needs to be regulated.

Investment Contract

As can be seen in the definition of a security recited above, there are many investments where the name of the investment clearly denotes them as securities. However, the term *investment contract* does not have a clear meaning. The business of group ownership of commercial and investment real estate falls under the security definition through this term.

No matter what legal entity a group chooses—tenant-in-common, general partnership, limited partnership, limited liability company, real estate investment trust—the application of the term investment contract must be understood so that we operate properly in the world of security laws.

Common language definition of an investment contract

An investment may be commonly defined as the placement of money or capital in some business in the expectation receiving income or profit. Income would be any gain or recurring benefit from operations. Profit would be the benefit or advantage coming from the conduct or sale of a business.

A contract may be commonly defined as the agreement between two or more persons to do or not do something.

Put together, an investment contract is an agreement between two or more persons to make an investment of money with the expectation of income or profit.

This interpretation of the term investment contract really creates a catch-all for unusual investments that are not categorized or specifically named in the definition of a security.

The Supreme Court defined an investment contract in Howey

In **SEC v. W.J. Howey Co., 328 U.S. 293 (1946),** the Court heard a case involving the sale of parcels of land in a citrus grove to investors over the period of February 1941 to May 1943. The Court was asked to rule the real estate investment plan a security because it was not simply a straight real estate purchase but an investment contract.

The Howey Co. owned large tracts of citrus acreage in Lake County, Florida. For several years, it planted about five hundred acres annually, keeping half of the groves for itself, and offering the other half to the public to generate cash to help it with the rest of its development. An affiliate, Howey-in-the-Hills Service, Inc.

was involved in cultivating and developing these groves, including harvesting and marketing the crops.

Each potential investor was offered a land sales contract from the Howey Co. and a service contract from Howey-in-the-Hills. The investors were told that it was not feasible to invest in the groves without a service contract. While the potential investor could hire other service companies in the area, 85% of the acreage sold during a three-year period was covered by service contracts with Howey-in-the-Hills.

During the three-year period, forty-two investors bought land in the groves. Thirty-one of the investors bought parcels that were less than five acres each. The average size was 1.33 acres and many sales were for less than an acre. When the purchaser chose the service contract from Howey-in-the-Hills, they granted the company a ten-year contract without the option of cancellation. For a specific fee plus the costs of labor and materials, the company was given full discretion and control over the cultivation, the harvest, and the marketing of the crops. All of the fruit was pooled and sold, and the investors received an allocation of the net profits.

The investors were for the most part non-residents of Florida. They were business and professional people who lacked the knowledge, skill, and equipment necessary to run the groves themselves.

Presumably, some of the buyers of the parcels were going to use the profits from operations to help them make the payments on the purchase of the parcels. The business in the citrus grove failed and investors lost their investments. The investors sued, claiming that what they were sold were unregistered securities in violation of the federal securities laws.

After review, the Court felt the facts demonstrated that what on the surface appeared to be simply the sales of individual parcels of real estate to individual investors was actually an investment contract because it stated that a security exists where:

> **...individuals were led to invest money in a common enterprise with the expectation they would earn a profit solely through the efforts of the promoter or of someone other than themselves.**

The facts showed the *investors had an assumption and expectation of receiving a profit without any active effort on their part*. The investors did not expect to use the land themselves but instead were attracted to the investment solely by the prospects of a return on their investment through the efforts of the Howey companies.

Howey test

An outcome of **Howey** was that the court established a four-prong test that has become the basis for determining what constitutes an investment contract under the federal securities laws. **Howey** is the test that will likely be used to determine if a group investment is considered a security.

The four factors are
> an investment of money;
> in a common enterprise;
> with the expectation of profits; and
> solely through the efforts of the promoter.

An investment of money

The issue of *an investment of money* is relatively easy to understand. When an investor invests cash or something of a value such as an irrevocable letter of credit or promissory note, the first factor in the test is met. The contribution of labor or a gift of money would not be considered an investment of money.

In a common enterprise

A corporation, real estate investment trust, limited partnership, limited liability company, general partnership, and some tenant-in-common relationships would certainly be considered to be a *common enterprise*.

A common enterprise need not have any written agreement, need not operate under a common name, or have any common ownership. A tenant-in-common ownership in investment real estate is an example of such an enterprise. One of the on-going issues in tenant-in-common ownership of investment real estate is whether the ownership arrangement is a common enterprise under the definition of an investment contract.

With the expectation of profits

Certainly, the definition of a profit should be clear. The investors would invest in an enterprise that would be run to make a profit and the investors would share in the profits of the enterprise. Profits can be differentiated from interest on a loan or when the investment is really a gift, and there may be no expectation of receiving a profit.

Solely through the efforts of the promoter

This factor is the one that gives real estate group sponsors a problem. In determining whether there is an investment contract and, as a result, a security, the most problematic words are *solely* through the promoter or *someone other than themselves*.

The question is always: Does the Court interpret solely as exclusively, mainly, or partly?

In **Howey**, the facts showed that, while it might have been possible for the investors to work the land they purchased or hire another service company, none of the investors intended to do any of the activities that would be needed to raise, harvest, and market the citrus. In fact, many of the investors were visiting Florida on vacation when they made the purchase and returned to their homes in other states. Any profit had to come solely from the efforts of the Howey-in-the-Hills Co., the operator of the groves. The facts in this case would be a clear example of the most restrictive meaning of the word "solely."

At the other end of the spectrum would be two people, each owning an undivided 50% interest in tenant-in-common ownership of a retail property where each investor participates equally in all management decisions and must sign each document, including all checks. While this is clearly an investment of money in a common enterprise with the expectation of a profit, the fourth factor is not present because the profits would not be produced *as a result of the efforts someone other than themselves*.

Most real estate owned by an investment group would fall somewhere in between these two extreme examples. While each situation is looked at through the specific facts, attorneys who litigate these actions with the SEC will state that 90% or more of the cases that get to court are determined to be securities.

*In **Howey**, the Court also painted a broad brush over what a security might be when it said the test for a security should be flexible and capable of being applied whenever people seek to use the money of others based on the promise of future profits.*

Prepurchase activities of the sponsor

In an effort to avoid the securities rules, investments could be structured by sponsors so that after the sponsors have put the transaction together, they sell the interests to investors and do not stay involved in the day-to-day management. This would be prevalent in the tenant-in-common industry, where the sponsor purchases the property, arranges long-term financing, obtains tenants, packages the investments, and then sells fractional interests to investors.

In **SEC v. Mutual Benefits Corp. (11ᵗʰ Cir. 2005) 408 FR.3d 737,** the court stated that significant prepurchase managerial activities may satisfy **Howey** if the promoters expended significant efforts in selecting the asset and negotiating the price of the asset in which the investors would acquire an interest. At the present time, the author knows of no case which addresses this issue in the area of real estate group ownership, but it is something that we should keep researching.

Other statements of the principles in Howey

The California Supreme Court has said that no list of investment vehicles would be as definitive as defining what a security is, but the courts must look to see whether the transaction falls within the regulatory purpose of the securities laws which is to protect the public against the imposition of unsubstantial, unlawful, and fraudulent investment schemes.

In **United Housing Foundation, Inc. v. Forman (1975) 421 U.S. 837,** the Supreme Court said the basis of the federal securities test is "the presence of an investment in a common venture premised on a reasonable expectation of profits to be derived from the entrepreneurial or managerial efforts of others." The Court said that profits meant "either capital appreciation resulting from the development of the initial investment…or a participation in earnings resulting from the use of investors' funds."

Limited partnerships vs. limited liability companies

The meaning of the word "solely" has great importance when discussing whether an interest in a limited partnership or a limited liability company is considered an investment contract. While a limited partner is restricted from any direct role in the management of the group, a member of a limited liability company may have the authority and ability to take an active role in management.

While it is generally accepted that interests of a limited partner are securities, it is a subject of some legal debate as to whether the interest of a group member in a limited liability company is a security. In fact, the federal securities rules do not state that an interest in a limited liability company *is not* a security.

Limited liability companies are created according to state law. The facts as to the rights and duties given to the members through the operating agreement must be examined to determine if the interests are deemed to be securities. The sponsor intending to use the limited liability company entity should review the state security rules on this issue, as some states have made the decision that an interest in a limited liability company, operating according to the state limited liability company act, is not *automatically* a security. Some states have not made any such determination.

Most interests in a limited liability company would not satisfy a literal reading of the word "solely" in that the members have the right to vote on a few major decisions. However, when the members *have little input* into the management of the group and depend *primarily* on the manager's efforts for any profits to be generated, it is likely the interests would be considered a security under the federal standards set in the **Howey** test.

In other limited liability companies where all the members are managers, the members take a direct and active involvement in the daily management, so that any profits or losses would likely be a result of the members' own actions within the company. These interests would probably not be considered a security under the federal standards set in the **Howey** test.

An example of one state's approach would be a case from the Arizona Appeals Court in **Nutek Information Systems, Inc. v. Arizona Corp. Comm., 977 P.2d 826 (Ct. App., AZ., 1998)** where the court ruled that while an interest in a limited liability company does not automatically constitute a security, each situation must be addressed on a case-by-case-basis. In the case reviewed, the Court found that most members of the limited liability company were *passive*, in they did not have managerial control. In addition, the contractual arrangement made it practically impossible for the members to replace the management and as such, the members had no meaningful control. The interests were deemed to be a security under Arizona security laws.

In a case in Texas, **Busse v Pacific Cattle Feeding Fund #1 LTD, 896 S.W.2d 807 (1995)** the court found a security exists

When an individual invests in an enterprise and the money invested is used to make a profit for the investor with limited involvement of the part of the investor.

How do you think that court would rule on the issue of the presence of a security interest, if a limited liability company had an operating agreement that gave the members little day-to-day management control, but gave them absolute authority and control over the group manager, including the absolute right of replacement *without cause*?

SEC v. Edwards

In January 2004, the U.S. Supreme Court ruled on a case, **SEC v. Edwards, 540 U.S. 389 (2004)** that may have implications to real estate being sold as securities. This case dealt with a payphone sale-leaseback program where 10,000 people invested approximately $300 million. ETS Payphones Inc., owned by Charles Edwards, who conducted significant prepurchase activities, sold payphones to the public and leased them back, installed the payphones, agreed to manage the payphones, entered into a repurchase agreement, and promised the investors a fixed rate of return. The payphones did not generate enough revenue to make the lease payment to the investors, and the company filed for bankruptcy. The investors contacted the SEC, and the SEC brought a civil action against the company for securities violations.

The investment in the payphones was offered for approximately $7,000. Purchasers were to receive $82 per month over the five year leaseback agreement, which equates to a 14% annual return. The purchasers were not involved with the day to day operations of the payphones. The company selected the site for the installation of the phones, installed the equipment, arranged for the connection and long distance service, collected the coin revenues, and maintained and repaired the phones. The buyback agreement called for the company to refund the full purchase price at the end of the lease or within 180 days of the investor's request.

The first court found the arrangement was an investment contract and applied the federal securities rules. Upon appeal, a second court reversed based on the fact the contract offered a *fixed rate of return rather than a profit* and the return was not derived solely from the efforts of others.

When the case reached the Supreme Court, the unanimous decision was the transactions were investment contracts and therefore securities. Justice Sandra Day O'Connor wrote the opinion and said that

> **the test for whether a particular scheme is an investment contract was established in our decision in SEC v. W.J. Howey Co.…We look to 'whether the scheme involves an investment of money in a common enterprise with profits to come solely from the efforts of others'…We hold that an investment scheme promising a fixed rate of return can be an 'investment contract' and thus a 'security' subject to the federal securities law.**

The argument made by Edwards was the contract delivered the income, not the people promoting the offering. The fact that the contract promised the investors a return *of* their money and a return *on* their money was enough for the Court to find that a profit existed. Regarding their new approach to the definition of what a profit is, the Court stated

> **There is no reason to distinguish between promises of fixed returns and promises of variable returns for purposes of the test, so understood. In both cases, the investing public is attracted by representations of investment income, as purchasers were in this case by ETS' invitation to "watch the profits add up."** **…Moreover, investments pitched as low-risk (such as those offering a "guaranteed" fixed return) are particularly attractive to individuals more vulnerable to investment fraud, including older and less sophisticated investors…unscrupulous marketers of investments could evade the securities laws by picking a rate of return to promise. We will not read into the securities laws a limitation not compelled by the language that would so undermine the laws' purposes.**

The Court put the test as another set of words when it said that

> **The "touchstone" of an investment contract is the presence of an investment in a common venture premised on a reasonable expectation of profits to be derived from the entrepreneurial or managerial efforts of others…**

Daniel S. Rosefelt, a Maryland attorney and CPA, who was present in the Court to hear the delivery of the opinion, believes that this decision can have an effect on real estate group ownership transactions, especially in tenant in common transactions. Here is his conclusion:

> **With regard to real estate tenant-in-common investment programs (TICs), the SEC v. Edwards's decision generally expands the reach of the federal securities laws for TICs being marketed as real estate investments with existing lease income/returns for the investor. TICs with sale-and-leaseback arrangements are clearly more vulnerable. The representations being made and actual control (or lack thereof) for the TIC investors, are all factors effecting the program's status as real estate or as a security. Sponsors, brokers, and investors should seek legal counsel well versed in TIC real estate securities law before promoting, selling, or investing in a non-security real estate.**

Examples of real estate investments that appear to be securities under Howey and Edwards

If the following investment interests were analyzed using the standards expressed in **Howey**, *they would likely be determined to be an investment contract* and, therefore, a security.

- A real estate broker or property manager attracts an investor from another state to invest money into a four-unit building based on the fact the broker will also invest in the property and will handle all of the decisions regarding the acquisition, management, and disposition of the property without any involvement of the investor who expects to make a profit from the activity.

- A husband and wife purchase an ownership interest in a condominium project in Hawaii where they are shown that resale prices of these condominiums and the value of similar condominium projects have been increasing. During the purchase process, the couple was told their condominium unit could be put in a rental pool with the other units and would be rented to vacationers so the cost of ownership could be offset by rental income.

- A senior citizen purchases two weeks in a timeshare hotel property in San Francisco. Some of the units have not been sold to the public, and the management company continues to run the project as a bed-and-breakfast. The management company performs all the management and rental activities of the property. As a promotional comment, the management company states that rental income of the bed-and-breakfast units will help offset the cost of the owner's units.

- An investor buys units in a limited partnership that is formed to buy a parcel of vacant land. The person who formed the partnership is a home builder who owns and is building on the adjacent land. The investor is told that, as soon as the home builder gets the entitlements, the lot sales and home building would begin, and the profit potential is substantial.

- A new doctor wants to open a practice in an established medical building. A requirement for all doctors practicing in the building is they must purchase an ownership interest in the building. Instead of paying rent, each doctor is charged a pro-rata share of the operating costs. A building management committee is made up of three doctors who built the building ten years ago and have all decision making authority. The building management committee hires a property management firm to handle all the accounting and building maintenance tasks.

Other ways laws deal with the security issues

As you read the examples above, you saw situations that you recognized as being governed by different sets of laws, such as state condominium laws and timeshare laws. Certain situations have demanded that states deal with real estate issues when complying with the federal securities rules would be cumbersome. But in certain situations, the federal securities rules must be reviewed and followed when applicable.

> *TIP: As an observation, many states allow single-investor limited liability companies. These would not be considered a security as there is no common enterprise, and the results are clearly dependent on the action of the only investor.*

Alternative approaches to the definition of a security

As the world of investment transactions and the application of securities law expand, there are different approaches that a real estate practitioner might encounter. Here are some examples.

Liberal meaning of the word "solely"

In **SEC v Glenn W. Turner Enterprises, Inc., 474 F.2d 476 (9th Cir 1973)** the 9th circuit court used a less literal approach to the word "solely." The court found that as long as someone other than the investor makes the *essential* managerial efforts that will ultimately determine the failure or success of an enterprise, an investment contract may still exist even if the investor is active in the enterprise and is not depending solely on the efforts of others for profit.

This situation could arise in a limited liability company where the members may have retained limited management responsibilities through the operating agreement but have granted the major decision-making power to the group sponsor. A sponsor should ask, "What is the amount of authority that needs be retained by the members so the investment is not considered an investment contract?" The answer to that question is likely to depend on a reading of the specific operating agreement in question.

Development of the theory of *risk capital*

Some states have developed an alternative theory of determining what constitutes a security by adopting the term risk capital as the standard by which an investment program may be deemed a security.

In its broadest application, risk capital would be applied to any situation where an investor invests money with the hope of some return in an enterprise over which the investor has no significant control. In the narrowest application, risk capital would be applied only when the investor is providing initial capitalization for a project or investing in an enterprise that puts the investor's capital subject to a high level of risk.

In **Howey**, a factor is that the investor expects to make a profit from the investment. It is likely the expectation of profit is the inducement to the investor to make their initial investment. In contrast, under the risk capital theory, expectation of profit is not a factor, but the simple fact the investors' capital is placed at risk in an enterprise determines the investment is a security. States that adopt a standard of simply placing capital at risk may apply a wider application of the securities law than the federal law has established.

One example of the application of the risk capital rule could be the sale of memberships in a golf course to be developed. The purchasers of the memberships most likely wanted to buy the membership for social and recreational goals and not with the expectation of profit. Under federal laws this would not be a security transaction. However, under California's application of the risk capital rule, the golf course membership could be determined to be a security in there is a possibility the club would never be completed. Money could be lost and, as such, the investors had placed their capital at risk.

On the other end of the risk capital standard would be the purchase of an interest in a group investment with a specified piece of raw land to be held as a long-term investment as the real estate asset. It would be possible that a court could hold that if an investor in a group investment receives the full value of their investment through a share of the ownership in the entity that owns the land no capital is placed at risk at that time. While it is possible the investor could lose money, it might be argued the events that would cause the loss of money are considered to be marketplace risks, not security risks.

> *TIP: Sponsors should be very attentive to the evolving theory of risk capital on the state level. On the one hand, the application of the theory could remove many group investments in specific properties from the application of state securities laws. On the other hand, the application of the theory could be such that it would bring almost all group investments under the application of state securities laws. This is one more of the risks that a sponsor accepts when they enter the group investment business.*

Anti- Fraud Provisions of the Securities Act

However, before we start to discuss the exemptions from full registration, you should keep in mind the availability of an exemption from full registration with the SEC does not allow an exemption from the anti-fraud provisions of the Securities Act. Generally there is not any means by which a sponsor can be exempt from the laws regarding fraud.

Jurisdiction remains with the SEC

When the securities have been offered, directly or indirectly, through the means of transportation or communications through interstate commerce, including the mail, telephone, Federal Express, UPS, fax transmissions, and the Internet, the securities laws state the SEC will maintain jurisdiction over the acts of the issuer even in the face of an offering that is otherwise exempt from registration.

Transactions involving use of mail are subject to Securities Act of 1933, whether or not the mail moved across state lines since the Act applies to both interstate and intrastate transactions when the issue of fraud is present. ***SEC v. Timetrust, Inc. (1939, DC Cal) 28 F Supp 34.***

Sales of individual interests in oil and gas leases came within registration provisions of Securities Act, where copies of documents of assignment were mailed to assignees and fraud was present in the offering. ***Moses v. Michael (1961, CA5 Miss) 292 F2d 614, 4 FR Serv 2d 282, 15 OGR 635.***
Allegation of the delivery of contract certificates through the mail was not alone sufficient, in the absence of fraudulent acts, to bring the offering under the Securities Act, but allegations of fraudulent acts committed through the use of the mail for sending notices for payments, prospectuses, bulletins, and financial

statements for purpose of inducing continuance of payments by purchaser were sufficient to bring an action under the federal securities rules.

Gross v. Independence Shares Corp. (1941, DC Pa) 36 F Supp 541.

Proper venue

The securities laws state the venue, the location of the court where the legal action will take place, will be determined by where the fraudulent acts occurred, where the transaction took place, or where the issuer lives.

Fraud in the offer or sale of securities

The securities laws override any exemption when it is alleged and proven an individual committed fraud in a securities transaction. Language in a complaint filed in a fraud action under the securities laws would look like this:

> **Defendant, who used transportation or communications in interstate commerce, including use of the mails:**
>
> **with forethought, employed devices and schemes to defraud;**
>
> **obtained money or property by means of untrue statements of a material fact or by omitting to state a material fact necessary in order to make the statements made, in light of the circumstances under which they were made, not misleading; or**
>
> **engaged in transactions, practices, or courses of business which operated or would operate as a fraud or deceit upon the purchaser.**

The remedies the court can impose

The court can order any or all of the following:

- A temporary restraining order and a preliminary injunction freezing the assets of all involved in the action and appointing a receiver over each entity involved
- Each individual to disgorge all ill-gotten gains from their illegal conduct along with prejudgment interest
- Each individual to pay civil penalties
- Jurisdiction be retained over all individuals so as to provide equitable relief for all parties who have been damaged

15 USC Sec. 77t(d)

(d) Money penalties in civil actions.

   (1) Authority of Commission. Whenever it shall appear to the Commission that any person has violated any provision of this *title [15 USCS § § 77a* et seq.], the rules or regulations thereunder, or a cease-and-desist order entered by the Commission pursuant to section 8A of this *title [15 USCS § 77h-1]*, other than by committing a violation subject to a penalty pursuant to section 21A of the Securities Exchange Act of 1934 [*15 USCS § 78u-1]*, the Commission may bring an action in a United States district court to seek, and the court shall have jurisdiction to impose, upon a proper showing, a civil penalty to be paid by the person who committed such violation.

   (2) Amount of penalty.

   (A) First tier. The amount of the penalty shall be determined by the court in light of the facts and circumstances. For each violation, the amount of the penalty shall not exceed the greater of (i) $ 5,000 for a natural person or $ 50,000 for any other person, or (ii) the gross amount of pecuniary gain to such defendant as a result of the violation.

   (B) Second tier. Notwithstanding subparagraph (A), the amount of penalty for each such violation shall not exceed the greater of (i) $ 50,000 for a natural person or $ 250,000 for any other person, or (ii) the gross amount of pecuniary gain to such defendant as a result of the violation, if the violation described in paragraph (1) involved fraud, deceit, manipulation, or deliberate or reckless disregard of a regulatory requirement.

   (C) Third tier. Notwithstanding subparagraphs (A) and (B), the amount of penalty for each such violation shall not exceed the greater of (i) $ 100,000 for a natural person or $ 500,000 for any other person, or (ii) the gross amount of pecuniary gain to such defendant as a result of the violation, if—

   (I) the violation described in paragraph (1) involved fraud, deceit, manipulation, or deliberate or reckless disregard of a regulatory requirement; and

(II) such violation directly or indirectly resulted in substantial losses or created a significant risk of substantial losses to other persons.

First tier

Based on the facts in the case, the court can ask for penalties by claiming a first tier penalty if the acts are relatively minor. The court can assign a specific amount of fine or a fine equal to the amount of gain they determine was obtained through the fraudulent act.

Second tier

A second tier penalty, which allows the court to ask for larger fixed amount penalties, can be requested when the court finds facts that the actions involved fraud, deceit, manipulation, or deliberate or reckless disregard of a regulatory requirement.

Third tier

The third tier penalty can be assessed when the facts indicate the actions involved fraud, deceit, manipulation, or deliberate or reckless disregard of a regulatory requirement, and the violation directly or indirectly resulted in substantial losses or created a significant risk of substantial losses to other persons.

Limited liability clauses will not protect you either

People often comment that when they are members of a limited liability company they have limited liability and feel they cannot be held responsible for their actions. While limited liability is a feature of a limited liability company, there is no limited liability on behalf of the manager who commits fraud against the investors. If it is shown the manager has committed fraud and then it is shown the transaction involved a security, the fraud provisions of the securities laws discussed here would likely apply.

Intrastate offerings under Rule 147

When all the actions of the group take place within one state, there may be an exemption from federal registration. This intrastate exemption is known commonly as a Rule 147 exemption.

Rule 147, found in the Securities Act of 1933, created an exemption from a full federal securities registration. This exemption is based on the Tenth Amendment to the Constitution of the United States that limits the rights of the federal government to regulate activities that take place entirely within the boundaries of one state. The intent behind the rule is to aid local efforts to raise capital without expensive regulations. The rule provides a sponsor with a safe harbor for complying with federal securities regulations.

An offering that would likely fall under Rule 147 will have each of these three factors present:

- The offering of the securities and sale of the securities are made only to investors who are residents of a single state.
- The group must have its principal office in that state.
- The group must be doing business in that state.

Rule 147 does not set any restrictions as to general solicitation or advertising but leaves that regulation up to the state in which the exemption is being sought. The rule contains no restrictions as to the dollar amount size of the offering as any such restriction would be up to the state.

Offerings may only be made to residents of the single state
The group sponsor must be certain that all offering of the securities are made only to individuals or entities that have their principal residence or place of business within the single state.

All the investors are from a single state
A written representation is required from the purchaser of the units that their principal residence is in the single state. Reselling units is prohibited for nine months after the sale of the last unit.

The office of the group is in the same state as the investors
Corporations must be incorporated in the state. General partnerships, limited partnerships, and limited liability companies must have their principal place of business in the state.

The business of the group must be conducted in the same state as the investors and the office of the group
To be considered as doing business in a state, at a minimum, 80% of the assets of the group must be located in the state, 80% of the revenues come from business conducted in the state, and 80% of the offering proceeds are used in the state.

Compliance is the responsibility of the sponsor
It is the responsibility of the sponsor of the group to assure the elements of Rule 147 are met.

An available defense to the charge of selling unregistered securities

A common element of a legal claim an investor would bring against a sponsor is if the sponsor sold unregistered securities in violation of federal securities laws. A valid defense to that claim would be that the securities were offered under the Intrastate Offering Exemption, based on meeting the elements of Rule 147. As such, the securities were exempt from the registration requirement of the Securities Act of 1933 and did not need to be registered.

Federal Preemption of State Laws

If a sponsor cannot operate under the intrastate exemption offered under Rule 147, then the sponsor must register their offering according to the federal securities rules, unless there is some exemption available. In addition, the sponsor must register their securities in each state where the securities are offered. The term *Blue Sky Rules* means the individual securities rules of each state. The sponsor could find themselves operating under the federal rules and the individual rules of each state. In effect, there are fifty-two sets of securities rules a sponsor would need to be aware of when each of the fifty states, the District of Columbia, and the federal rules are counted. These multiple rules created a situation that was not conducive to capital formation.

National Securities Markets Improvement Act of 1996 (NSMIA)

The National Securities Markets Improvement Act of 1996 (Improvement Act) was adopted to try to solve the problem of multiple securities laws and multiple jurisdiction claims. NSMIA's main provision is to allow the federal government to preempt the state laws on certain securities transactions.

Basically, NSMIA says that state securities regulators are preempted from most regulations of securities offered in reliance on Reg. D. Rule 506, which is discussed later in this section. The federal rules take precedence, and no state can impose their own rules on the securities. The sponsor, anticipating an offering that is not exempt under the intrastate exemption in Rule 147, must research each state where the securities are being offered to see if those states have embraced NSMIA.

Let's look at the scope of the law. First, no state rule requiring registration of a security may be applied to a *covered* security or one that *will be covered* upon completion of the offering. Secondly, it says the states cannot impose any requirements on the offering document used in a covered security. Lastly, it prohibits the states from imposing requirements on the issuer of a covered security.

Section 18—Exemption from State Regulation of Securities Offerings

a.   **Scope of Exemption**

Except as otherwise provided in this section, no law, rule, regulation, or order, or other administrative action of any State or any political subdivision thereof—

1. requiring, or with respect to, registration or qualification of securities, or registration or qualification of securities transactions, shall directly or indirectly apply to a security that—

A. is a covered security; or

B. will be a covered security upon completion of the transaction;

2.   shall directly or indirectly prohibit, limit, or impose any conditions upon the use of--

A. with respect to a covered security described in subsection (b), any offering document that is prepared by or on the behalf of the issuer; or

B. any proxy statement, report to shareholders, or other disclosure document relating to a covered security or the issuer thereof that is required to be and is filed with the Commission or any national thereof that is required to be and is filed with the Commission or any national securities organization registered under section 15A of the Securities Exchange Act of 1934, except that this subparagraph does not apply to the laws, rules, regulations, or orders, or other administrative actions of the State of incorporation of the issuer; or

3.   shall directly or indirectly prohibit, limit, or impose conditions, based on the merits of such offering or issuer, upon the offer or sale of any security described in paragraph (1).

The Improvement Act then goes on to establish what a covered security would be. The first category identifies securities that are nationally traded securities. The second category is that of an investment company. A third category of a covered security is established as a security sold to qualified purchasers, which is the same as an accredited investor, which will be explained more fully later in this section. The last category covers securities that are exempt from registration under various rules.

b.   **Covered Securities**

For the purposes of this section, the following are covered securities:

1.   Exclusive federal registration of nationally traded securities.

A security is a covered security if such security is—

A.   listed, or authorized for listing, on the New York Stock Exchange or the American Stock Exchange, or listed, or authorized for listing, on the National Market System of the NASDAQ Stock Market (or any successor to such entities);

B.   listed, or authorized for listing, on a national securities exchange (or tier or segment thereof) that has listing standards the Commission determines by rule (on its own initiative or on the basis of a petition) are substantially similar to the listing standards applicable to securities describe in subparagraph (A); or

C.   is a security of the same issuer that is equal in seniority or that is a senior security to a security described in subparagraph (A) or (B).

2.   Exclusive federal registration of investment companies.

A security is a covered security if such security is a security issued by an investment company that is registered, or that has filed a registration statement, under the Investment Company Act of 1940.

3. **Sales to qualified purchasers.**

A security is a covered security with respect to the offer or sale of the security to qualified purchasers, as defined by the Commission by rule. In prescribing such rule, the Commission may define the term "qualified purchaser" differently with respect to different categories of securities, consistent with the public interest and the protection of investors.

4. **Exemption in connection with certain exempt offerings.**

A security is a covered security with respect to a transaction that is exempt from registration under this title pursuant to—

A. paragraph (1) or (3) of section 4, and the issuer of such security files reports with the Commission pursuant to section 13 or 15(d) of the Securities Exchange Act of 1934;

B section 4(4);

C. section 3(a), other than the offer or sale of a security that is exempt from such registration pursuant to paragraph (4), (10) or (11) of such section, except that a municipal security that is exempt from such a registration pursuant to paragraph (2) of such section is not a covered security with respect to the offer or sale of such security in the State in which the issuer of such security is located; or

D. Commission rules or regulations issued under section 4(2), except that this subparagraph does not prohibit a State from imposing notice filing requirements that are substantially similar to those required by rule or regulation under section 4(2) that are in effect on September 1, 1996.

Paragraph D, immediately above, refers to the private placement regulations under Regulation D, which will be discussed later in this section.

The following section states that even though NSMIA prohibits the state from imposing its restrictions on covered offerings, the state can still exert authority by requiring the issuer to file a notice and pay fees to the state. In addition, the state can prosecute parties if fraudulent activities are conducted against its citizens.

c.   Preservation of Authority.

1.   Fraud authority.

Consistent with this section, the securities commission (or agency or office performing like functions) of any State shall retain jurisdiction under the laws of such State to investigate and bring enforcement actions with respect to fraud or deceit, or unlawful conduct by a broker or dealer, in connection with securities or securities transactions.

2.   Preservation of filing requirements.

A. Notice filings permitted.

Nothing in this section prohibits the securities commission (or any agency or office performing like functions) of any State from requiring the filing of any document filed with the Commission pursuant to this title, together with annual or periodic reports of the value of securities sold or offered to be sold to persons located in the State (if such sales data is not included in documents filed with the Commission), solely for notice purposes and the assessment of any fee, together with a consent to service of process and any required fee.

B.   Preservation of fees

i.   In general

Until otherwise provided by law, rule, regulation, or order, or other administrative action of any State, or any political subdivision thereof, adopted after the date of enactment of the National Securities Markets Improvement Act of 1996, filing or registration fees

with respect to securities or securities transactions shall continue to be collected in amounts determined pursuant to State law as in effect on the day before such date.

ii. Schedule

The fees required by this subparagraph shall be paid, and all necessary supporting data on sales or offers for sales required under subparagraph (A), shall be reported on the same schedule as would have been applicable had the issuer not relied on the exemption provided in subsection (a).

Most practical application of NSMIA

The most likely application of this law to sponsors of real estate group investments will be when the offering conforms to Rule 506 of Regulation D. This rule will be explained in the following section, but, in summary, it will be a private placement made only to accredited or other qualified investors.

Loss of the Rule 506 exemption results not only in the loss of the federal exemption but will subject the security to full registration, not only on the federal level but possibly also on the state level.

Private Placement Exemptions to the Securities Act of 1933

While the general rule is that all securities offerings must be registered with the SEC, the SEC does not have sufficient manpower to regulate and police every group investment that meets the definition of a security. In addition, it is recognized that many investments that are securities involve small amounts of money and investors who know each other and know the business that is the subject of the investment. As a result, the SEC has established exemptions from full registration for *private* placements of securities, while requiring the full registration of all *public* offerings of securities.

Regulation D of the Securities Act of 1933 (Reg. D)

Reg. D establishes the rules under which a sponsor will likely conduct their group investment business when the group is conducting business across state lines and therefore is not exempt from registration under Rule 147. The exemptions to full registration apply to offerings that are determined to be private placements, rather than public offerings.

Public vs. *private* according to SEC

The term *public offering* is not defined in the Securities Act of 1933. The SEC initially indicated the following factors should be considered when determining if an offer is private or public: *Source: Securities Act Release No. 33-285 (January 24, 1935)*

- The number of offerees and their relationship with each other and the sponsor
- The number of securities offered
- The size of the offering
- The manner of the offering

Private placements according to the U.S. Supreme Court

In 1953, almost twenty years after the establishment of the SEC, the Court issued their only interpretation of private placements. The court felt the purpose of the securities rule is to "protect investors by promoting full disclosure of information thought necessary to informed investment decisions." The Court stated the question to be asked when determining if the offering is private is *whether the particular class of investor needs the protection* offered in the securities law **SEC v Ralston Purina Co., 346 U.S. 119(1953)**.

Not every investor needs protection

The SEC is charged with enforcing the Securities Act of 1933 to protect the public, but as a practical matter, the laws are designed to concentrate on large security offerings offered through the national, public financial markets such as the New York Stock Exchange. The exemptions discussed in this book will likely involve the majority of the smaller offerings the normal commercial and investment professional would sponsor.

The SEC does not have the staffing or financial resources to regulate every security issued throughout the United States offered to investors in smaller, private offerings where the investors have the ability to protect themselves because of their economic situation or educational level.

A valid defense

A valid defense to a claim of selling unregistered securities can be made by completing an offering in accordance with private placement exemptions available under Reg. D.

Sponsors who avail themselves with exemptions offered in Reg. D are not exempt from anti-fraud, civil liability, or other provisions of the federal securities laws, only the requirement of registration.

In addition, the application of the exemptions found in Reg. D does not free the sponsor from complying with applicable state law relating to the offer and sale of securities.

Accredited Investors Do Not Need Protection

The accredited investor concept was created in 1979 based on categories of investors who are able to obtain information on which to make an informed decision. Accredited investors, based on objective criteria indicating financial sophistication and ability to fend for themselves, do not require the protections of registration under the federal securities laws. The objective criteria dealt with financial sophistication, net worth, knowledge, experience in financial matters the amount of assets under management. These investors are also referred to as *qualified* under NSMIA, discussed above. As you will see, investors who are *rich* or *smart* are deemed not to need protection as long as they are provided with full disclosure of information needed to be able to make an informed decision.

Accredited individual investors

There are eight categories of accredited investors defined in **Regulation D, Rule 501 of the Securities Act.** The one definition that is of most importance to real estate sponsors would be the one that applies to individual investors. Portions of Rule 501 are included here:

> **(a) *Accredited investor. Accredited investor* shall mean any person who comes within any of the following categories, or who the issuer reasonably believes comes within any of the following categories, at the time of the sale of the securities to that person:**

> **(5) Any natural person whose individual net worth, or joint net worth with that person's spouse, exceeds $1,000,000.**

> **(i) Except as provided in paragraph (a)(5)(ii) of this section, for purposes of calculating net worth under this paragraph (a)(5):**

> **(A) The person's primary residence shall not be included as an asset;**

> **(B) Indebtedness that is secured by the person's primary residence, up to the estimated fair market**

value of the primary residence at the time of the sale of securities, shall not be included as a liability (except that if the amount of such indebtedness outstanding at the time of sale of securities exceeds the amount outstanding 60 days before such time, other than as a result of the acquisition of the primary residence, the amount of such excess shall be included as a liability); and

(C) Indebtedness that is secured by the person's primary residence in excess of the estimated fair market value of the primary residence at the time of the sale of securities shall be included as a liability;

(ii) Paragraph (a)(5)(i) of this section will not apply to any calculation of a person's net worth made in connection with a purchase of securities in accordance with a right to purchase such securities, provided that:

(A) Such right was held by the person on July 20, 2010;

(B) The person qualified as an accredited investor on the basis of net worth at the time the person acquired such right; and

(C) The person held securities of the same issuer, other than such right, on July 20, 2010.

(6) Any natural person who had an individual income in excess of $200,000 in each of the two most recent years or joint income with that person's spouse in excess of $300,000 in each of those years and has a reasonable expectation of reaching the same income level in the current year;

As the rule says, there are two ways an individual can be determined to meet the definition of being accredited, by net worth or by annual income.

The net worth requirement is $1 million, but the investor cannot count the equity in their primary residence in calculating their net worth. In addition, if the loans on the investor's primary residence are greater than the value of the primary residence, the amount by which the loans exceed the value must be counted as a liability in calculating the overall net worth.

The annual income requirement is $200,000 annually for the last two years if the investor is filing as an individual. If the couple is filing a joint tax return, the annual limit is $300,000. The income must reasonably be expected to meet the appropriate level in the year the investment is being made.

In addition, if the investor met the requirement of being accredited when the original investment was made in an offering, they would be considered to be accredited in the event any future investment would need to be made in this same offering, as when a capital call is required.

TIP: Prior to the passage of the Dodd-Frank Wall Street Reform and Consumer Protection Act in 2010, the equity in an investor's primary residence could be counted in the net worth calculation of an investor. The elimination of the ability to use that equity caused a large number of investors who were once considered to be accredited to no longer meet the net worth requirement. The effect of this change was felt more strongly in the parts of the country where housing was expensive. In many situations, group sponsors are now concentrating on getting investors qualified as accredited through the annual income test and ignoring the net worth test.

Accredited entities

Often a group sponsor will have entities approach them wishing to invest in their offerings. Entities can also meet the requirement of being accredited. The most common entities that a real estate sponsor will encounter that would meet the definition of accredited would be either of the following:

- Any trust, with total assets in excess of $5 million, not formed for the specific purpose of acquiring the securities offered, whose purchase is directed by a sophisticated person
- Any entity in which all of the equity owners are accredited investors. The equity owners may be either individuals or other entities as long as each meet the definition of accredited

Non-accredited investors need protection

Individuals or entities that do not meet the definition of accredited investor are classified as non-accredited investors. Non-accredited investors, along with investors who are given inadequate information or, as members of the public, are attracted to the investment opportunity through advertising or general solicitation, are deemed to need the protection of the federal securities laws.

Who is responsible for determining whether an investor is accredited?

The sponsor's responsibility

The sponsor is responsible to review subscription documents to ensure the accuracy and completeness of the documents and to determine the investor meets the suitability standards set for the offering. The investor must actually be accredited or the sponsor must have a reasonable basis for believing an investor is accredited at the time of an investment. When we read about Rule 506(b) and Rule 506(c), we will see some differences in the sponsor's responsibility.

The investor's responsibility

The investor is responsible for understanding whether they are accredited and for filling out the offering questionnaire accurately and completely. Most subscription agreements contain provisions whereby the investors agree to defend and or reimburse the issuer for any damage or liability incurred as a result of false information the investor provides in the subscription documents.

General Solicitation of Investors Is Not Allowed in Certain Private Offerings

A fundamental basis for the creation of the private placement exemption is that there has been no advertising or general solicitation for the sale of the securities made to members of the public. When there is no advertising or general solicitation, it is likely the investors have some preexisting relationship with the sponsor and, possibly, the other investors, and it is felt there is less need for the protection offered through full registration of the securities.

General solicitation rule prior to the JOBS Act

Prior to the JOBS Act (The Jumpstart Our Business Startups Act of 2012) made effective in September 2013 with the issuance of temporary regulations from the SEC, every security offered to members of the public by means of a general solicitation was required to be registered with the SEC and, most likely, with every state in which the securities are offered, unless there was some exemption.

Now, advertising and general solicitation became legal as a result of the JOBS Act, but the vast majority of private placements still operate under the prohibition of advertising or general solicitation. So a complete understanding of the prohibition against advertising and general solicitation is important to a group sponsor.

US Mail and interstate commerce

Every security offering that uses the US mail or other means of interstate commerce to solicit investments from the public must be registered unless there is some exemption available. The use of any communication methods deemed to be part of interstate commerce will be defined as general solicitation.

Use of various media

Any advertising, article, notice, or other communication published in any newspaper, magazine, or similar media or broadcast over television or radio shall be considered a general solicitation if it is determined the communication promotes the sale of a security to members of the public.

Use of seminars

Any seminar or meeting where the members of the public have been invited to attend, where a specific investment offering is promoted, would be considered a general solicitation. The holding of a meeting or seminar where no specific offering is promoted appears to be allowed based on the information coming from a no-action letter issued by the SEC relating to an Internet posting, as discussed below.

Rule regarding the use of the Internet

The general rule is that any posting of an *offering* of securities on a Web site is deemed to be a general solicitation.

Exception to the rule regarding the use of the Internet

An exception to this rule was made for the situation where there was an online prequalification of accredited investors, who, after their qualification, were issued private passwords to allow them to see the notification of a private placement on a Web site. **Source: SEC Letter of No Action, IPONET (avail. July 26, 1996)**

The business practice of the company was that it placed generic information on its Web site regarding the methods and benefits of investing in an Initial Public Offering (IPO). They advertised to attract members of the public to their Web site to view the generic information of investing in an IPO.

When a visitor to their Web site expressed interest in investigating the area of IPO investing, an offering questionnaire was emailed to the visitor. Upon completion of the questionnaire, the information was reviewed by the company to determine if the potential investor met the definition of an accredited investor and also met the specific suitability standards the company had established for their offerings.

As an additional step, a representative of the company made personal telephonic contact with the potential investor to confirm the information which had been provided. Only after these steps were taken to qualify the investor did the company offer information to the potential investor on a specific IPO.

The potential investor was then given a secure password with a specific date stamp and expiration date. Using the password, the potential investor could go online to view offering material on an IPO determined as being suitable for the investor. The investor could then complete the purchase of the security online.

After reviewing the facts, the SEC issued a letter saying they would take no action against this company and its marketing approach.

Discussion of NASD Notice to Members

In March 2005, the NASD (now FINRA), the organization that governs the action of licensed securities representatives and often works in connection with the SEC, issued **NASD Notice to Members 05-18** that deals with the issue of solicitation of investors, specifically in the tenant-in-common industry but gives sponsors of group investments instruction as to how to attract investors without violating the rules on solicitation. The section of this document that deals with solicitation is included here.

> **Members have requested guidance with regard to two specific methods of solicitation or advertising. In the first scenario, a registered representative who also holds a real estate license solicits potential investors by advertising a "real estate" seminar. At the seminar, investors are given a presentation on TIC exchanges and are made aware the member offers TIC investments to its customers. Since the advertisement for the seminar would be a general solicitation, and since the references to the TIC investments currently being offered by members would be deemed an offer of those securities, the members engaged in such offerings would not be able to rely on the exemption from registration for private placements under Regulation D.**

In the second scenario, members place advertisements in newspapers and magazines that indicate the member sells TIC interests, but the advertisements do not identify any particular TIC investment for sale by the member. Since the advertisement itself is a general solicitation, the issue for members is whether the advertisement includes an offer of securities. In general, such an advertisement would not be deemed an offer of securities if:

(a) the advertisement is generic;

(b) the advertisement is not being made in contemplation of an offering; and

(c) the member has procedures to ensure that an investor solicited via the advertisement will not be offered TICs the member is currently offering or contemplating offering at the time of the initial contact.

Advertisements that do not meet each of these three bullet point conditions are likely to be deemed general solicitations and inconsistent with the conditions for private placements conducted in compliance with Regulation D. Moreover, in addition to meeting these conditions, the other requirements under Regulation D also must be met, including establishing an adequate, substantive, and preexisting relationship with the investor and completing a suitability analysis prior to offering TICs to an investor.

Direction offered by the Notice

The three bullet points in this section of the Notice are really the key in directing the group sponsor in the correct actions to take in soliciting investors, whether through seminars or other forms of advertising.

Most real estate agents reading this book are used to marketing real estate to the public through various means of advertising to attract investors that are not known to the agent. In selling investors direct ownership in a property, there are no restrictions against this type of advertising. However, when selling ownership in a group, through what might be determined to be a security, there are restrictions.

It appears that, following the advice given in the Notice, a generic advertisement or seminar to attract investors who are not known to the sponsor would be allowed if there are no direct offerings or sales of securities made through the advertisement or at the seminar. If the advertisement or attendance at a seminar results in a sponsor-making contact with a potential investor, the advice is that the sponsor keep records to make sure the investor does not invest in an offering that is available at that time or an offering that is being contemplated at that time.

Seminars or other general solicitation to those with whom there is no substantive preexisting relationship may only be made with the intention of building a potential client base. Offers and sales of securities to those prospects identified through a general solicitation may only be made, i) after a substantive preexisting relationship has been established, ii) of a product that became available after the establishment of the relationship, and iii) that was not contemplated at the time the establishment of the relationship.

Discussions that would appear to be generic would seem to include:

- Discussions of the Internal Revenue Code
- Reference material on real estate investing not referencing a specific offer or sponsor
- LLC or TIC ownership concepts that do not mention an offering or sponsor

Two questions the sponsor should answer

When the offering is finally made to the investor, it appears that two questions must be able to be answered in the affirmative:

- Does the investor know enough about the sponsor so they can make an informed decision as to whether they want to make an investment in a program offered by the sponsor?
- Does the sponsor know the investor meets the suitability standard the sponsor has set for this offering and is this offering the type of offering in which the sponsor believes the investor would be interested?

It appears that if the sponsor could answer yes to the above questions, there must be a relationship established between the investors and the sponsor so the offer is not being made as a result of a solicitation, but as the result of an established business relationship.

The act of making an offer to an investor is not a solicitation per se, and, in the federal law, there are no limits as to the number of offers made, only to the number of investors. However, making an offer as a result of a solicitation is the action that is regulated.

Pre-suitability Questionnaire

A Pre-suitability Questionnaire asks questions that will help the sponsor determine if the investor meets the suitability requirements the sponsor usually sets for their group investments, allows the sponsor to learn of the past investment experience of the potential investor, and establishes the date the sponsor met the prospective investor. The establishment of the date is important, as the prospective investor cannot purchase units in an offering the sponsor has available on that date or is contemplating as of that date.

> *TIP: With the prior approval of your attorney, seminars and meetings where a generic presentation of the benefits of real estate investing and a presentation of the generic issues involved in group investing may be conducted in a manner that will not be considered general solicitation. After the meeting or seminar, it may be possible to qualify interested attendees as accredited investors who meet the suitability standards of your offering by using such a questionnaire.*

Integration

The concept of the integration of offerings was developed to prevent a sponsor from avoiding registration requirements by breaking one single larger offering into several smaller offerings for the purpose of claiming that each single offering was exempt from registration.

Integration defined

The SEC has issued a five-factor test to determine whether separate offerings should be integrated. **Source: SEC release No. 33-4552, 1962**
The five factors are whether or not

- the offerings are part of a single plan of financing
- the offerings involve issuance of the same class of security
- the offerings are made at or about the same time
- the same type of consideration is to be received
- the offerings are for the same general purpose

An example of a securities offering that may well be subject to integration

The first offering is a limited liability company established to raise cash to purchase a property that needs extensive renovation. A mortgage will be obtained to complete the purchase.

Three months later, a second offering, also a limited liability company, is made to raise the cash needed to complete the extensive renovation of the property. No additional financing will be obtained to aid in the completion of the renovation.

Through the application of the theory of integration, it is possible that both of these offerings will be considered part of the same offering. As a result, the private placement status of the offering may be jeopardized.

Three Private Placements Exemptions Available Under Reg. D

Most sponsors of group investments would like to be exempt from full federal registration but do not meet the requirements under the intrastate exemption because either the property being syndicated or at least one of the investors is from a different state than the state where the sponsor lives. So, as a result, they must cross state lines and when they do so, their offering falls under federal jurisdiction. The Securities Act of 1933 contains Regulation D (Reg. D). Today, Reg. D includes four rules (Rule 504, Rule 505, and Rule 506(b) and 506(c) (created through the JOBS Act) that address the areas of exemption from registration available to sponsors who offer securities while crossing state lines.

Reg. D. Rule 504: Offering not to exceed $1 million allowing unlimited accredited investors

Under **Reg. D. Rule 504, Reg. § 203.504**, the offering and sales of securities are exempt from federal registration if:

- The aggregate offering price of securities shall not exceed $1 million less the aggregate offering price for all securities within the twelve months before the start of and during the offering of these securities.
- Sales may be made to an unlimited number of accredited investors.
- General solicitation and general advertising is permitted only if the state or states in which the security is offered allows it.
- The offering cannot be a blind pool.

The Rule 504 exemption is available to the sponsor who wishes to form an investment group raising $1 million from an unlimited number of accredited investors. The offering must be a specific property offering. This is a typical investment group that might be formed by many sponsors. A similar offering could be made each twelve months.

Example of the calculation of aggregate offering price under Rule 504

In June, a sponsor sold $1 million of securities under the Rule 504 exemption in their first offering. In December of the same year, the sponsor wishes to sell an additional $800,000 of securities in another offering, under the Rule 504 exemption. The effect of the integration rule is the sponsor may not take advantage of Rule 504 for the December offering and must wait until the June of the next year, when the sponsor could sell up to $1 million of securities under Rule 504.

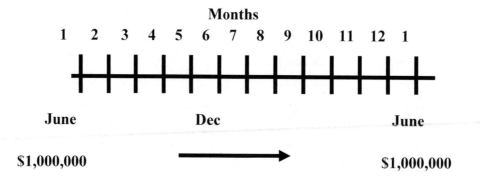

Reg. D Rule 505: Offering not to exceed $5 million allowing up to thirty-five non-accredited investors plus unlimited accredited investors

Under **Rule 505, Reg. § 230.505**, the offerings and sales of securities are exempt from federal registration if:

- The number of non-accredited investors shall not exceed thirty-five.
- The aggregate offering price of securities shall not exceed $5 million during a twelve-month period.
- No general solicitation or general advertising is permitted.
- There may be unlimited number of accredited investors.

The Rule 505 exemption is available to the sponsor who wishes to form an investment group raising $5 million from an unlimited number of accredited investors and thirty-five or fewer non-accredited investors. The offering could be a specific, a semi-specific, or blind pool offering. This is a typical investment group that might be formed by many sponsors. A similar offering could be made each twelve months.

Example of the calculation of aggregate offering price under Rule 505

In June, a sponsor offered and sold $3 million of securities under the Rule 505 exemption in their first offering. In December of the same year, the sponsor wished to offer an additional $3 million of securities in another offering under the Rule 505 exemption. The effect of the integration rule will be the sponsor would be limited to offering and selling only $2 million of securities in December. In June of the next year, the sponsor may offer another $3 million under Rule 505.

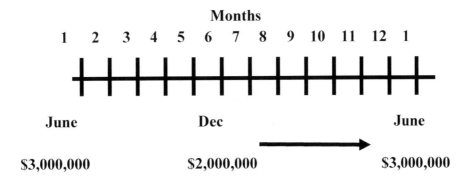

Reg. D Rule 506(b): Offerings without regard to dollar amount prohibiting advertising and general solicitation

Under **Rule 506, Reg. § 203.506**, no maximum dollar amount is established for the offerings and sales of securities. Under the terms of this rule, offerings are exempt from federal registration under the following conditions:

- There may be an unlimited number of accredited investors.
- The number of sophisticated investors shall not exceed thirty-five.
- Sophisticated investors are defined in Rule 506(b) as:
  Each purchaser who is not an accredited investor, either alone or with his purchaser representative(s) has such knowledge and experience in financing and business matters that he is capable of evaluating the merits and risks of the prospective investments, or the issuer reasonably believes immediately prior to making any sale that such purchaser comes within this description
- No general solicitation or general advertising is permitted.

A sponsor would use the exemption available under Rule 506(b) for any size offering but must use either 506(b) or 506(c) if they wanted to offer and raise more than $5 million. Under 506(b) a sponsor could raise money from thirty-five or fewer sophisticated investors and an unlimited number of accredited investors. If the sponsor limited the sale of securities to accredited investors, there would be no limit to the number of investors and no limit to the amount of money they could raise, as long as no general solicitation was used to attract investors.

Example of the calculation of aggregate offering price under Rule 506(b) and 505

In June, a sponsor offered and sold $3 million of securities under the Rule 506(b) exemption in their first offering. In December of the same year, the sponsor wishes to offer an additional $2 million of securities in another offering under the Rule 505 exemption. It appears the effect of the integration rule will be the sponsor would be able to offer and sell the $2 million of securities in December. Even if the aggregate offering price were determined to be $5 million, the total of both offerings, as long as there were no more than a total of thirty-five sophisticated and unaccredited investors, the offering would fall under Rule 505, which allows $5 million of funds to be raised.

It appears that in June of the next year the sponsor may offer another $3 million as long as the offering is conducted under Rule 505, and between the $2 million raised in December and the $3 million raised in June there are no more than a total of thirty-five unaccredited investors.

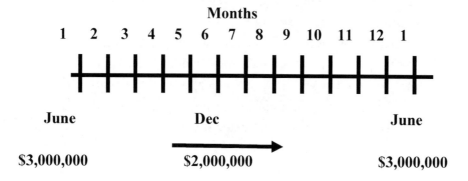

The Rule 506(b) exemption is available to the sponsor who wishes to form an investment group raising an unlimited amount of money from an unlimited number of accredited investors and thirty-five or fewer sophisticated investors. The offering could be a specific, a semi-specific, or blind pool offering. This is the type of investment group that is formed by most sponsors.

Reg. D Rule 506(c): Offerings without regard to dollar amount permitting the use of advertising and general solicitation

Section 201(a) of the JOBS Act requires the SEC to eliminate the prohibition on using general solicitation under Rule 506 where all purchasers of the securities are accredited investors and the issuer takes reasonable steps to verify that the purchasers are accredited investors.

To implement Section 201(a), the SEC adopted paragraph (c) of Rule 506. Under Rule 506(c), issuers can offer securities through means of general solicitation, provided that

all purchasers in the offering are accredited investors;

the issuer takes reasonable steps to verify their accredited investor status; and

certain other conditions in Regulation D are satisfied.

The Rule 506(c) exemption is available to the sponsor who wishes to form an investment group raising an unlimited amount of money from an unlimited number of accredited investors. The offering could be a specific, a semi-specific, or blind pool offering. This is the type of investment group that is formed by most sponsors. The rules on integration would be the same as under Rule 506(b).

The SEC has provided a guide to help issuers comply with the requirement that they "take steps to be reasonably assured" that all purchasers in a Rule 506(c) offering are accredited. The guide can be found at the link shown below, but its important parts are provided here: http://www.sec.gov/info/smallbus/secg/general-solicitation-small-entity-compliance-guide.htm.

The JOBS Act requires that issuers wishing to engage in general solicitation take "reasonable steps" to verify the accredited investor status of purchasers. Rule 506(c) sets forth a principles-based method of verification which requires an objective determination by the issuer (or those acting on its behalf) as to whether the steps taken are "reasonable" in the context of the particular facts and circumstances of each purchaser and transaction. Among the factors that an issuer should consider under this principles-based method are:

• the nature of the purchaser and the type of accredited investor that the purchaser claims to be;

• the amount and type of information that the issuer has about the purchaser; and

• the nature of the offering, such as the manner in which the purchaser was solicited to participate in the

offering, and the terms of the offering, such as a minimum investment amount.

In addition to this flexible, principles-based method, Rule 506(c) includes a non-exclusive list of verification methods that issuers may use, but are not required to use, when seeking greater certainty that they satisfy the verification requirement with respect to natural person purchasers. This non-exclusive list of verification methods consists of:

a. verification based on income, by reviewing copies of any Internal Revenue Service form that reports income, such as Form W-2, Form 1099, Schedule K-1 of Form 1065, and a filed Form 1040;

b. verification on net worth, by reviewing specific types of documentation dated within the prior three months, such as bank statements, brokerage statements, certificates of deposit, tax assessments and a credit report from at least one of the nationwide consumer reporting agencies, and obtaining a written representation from the investor;

c. a written confirmation from a registered broker-dealer, an SEC-registered investment adviser, a licensed attorney or a certified public accountant stating that such person or entity has taken reasonable steps to verify that the purchaser is an accredited investor within the last three months and has determined that such purchaser is an accredited investor; and

d. a method for verifying the accredited investor status of persons who had invested in the issuer's Rule 506(b) offering as an accredited investor before September 23, 2013 and remain investors of the issuer.

Rule 506(b) remains unchanged following the adoption of Rule 506(c) and continues to be available for issuers that wish to conduct a Rule 506 offering without the use

**of general solicitation or that do not wish to limit sales
of securities in the offering to accredited investors.**

Crowdfunding

Title III of the JOBS Act (interestingly entitled the "Capital Raising Online While Deterring Fraud and Unethical Non-Disclosure Act of 2012") will allow sponsors to use the Internet and social media to raise up to $1 million of securities in a twelve-month period. There is no limit to the number of investors in an offering, but there are limits on the amount of money one investor can invest with a single issuer based on:

- The greater of $2,000 or five percent (5%) of the investor's annual income or net worth, so long as each such investor's annual income or net worth is less than $100,000; or
- If the investor's annual income or net worth is equal to or more than $100,000, ten percent (10%) of the investor's annual income or net worth, not to exceed a maximum aggregate of $100,000 of securities sold.

Any crowdfunding transaction must be conducted using a broker or *funding portal* and the issuer of the securities must:

- Disclose the names of directors and officers and each investor who owns more than 20% of the issuer
- Provide a description of the business and business plan of the issuer
- Provide income tax returns for the issuer covering the previous year and financial statements of the issuer certified by the principal executive of the issuer, or financial statements reviewed by an independent public accountant; or audited financial statements, depending on the amount of the money to be raised in the offering
- Provide a statement of sources and uses of proceeds
- Other information the SEC prescribes for the protection of the investors

Additionally, the issuer may not sell the securities themselves, outside of the broker or the funding portal and must file annual reports with the SEC.

> *TIP: After an almost three-year wait, the SEC has yet to issue any proposed regulations on crowdfunding and actually has a posting on their Web site that crowdfunding is currently illegal. I feel that this rule will be of little use to our clients, as most clients want to raise their money, in an inexpensive way without the involvement of a broker dealer (funding portal) and that, in most markets, the limitation of a $1 million maximum raise makes this rule unusable for real estate syndication. In addition, some commentators say that until there is additional legislation, perhaps in the form of JOBS ACT II, the SEC will never issue regulations authorizing crowdfunding as established in the JOBS ACT.*

The current use of crowdfunding

There seems to be no trademark associated with the use of the word crowdfunding, and we hear a lot about it today. Many people say they are running crowdfunding platforms for real estate investing. Below are some of the early Web sites that call themselves crowdfunding sites and have been used by our clients.

www.Realtymogul.com

www.CrowdStreet.com

www.RealCrowd.com

The earliest use of crowdfunding I have come across in the United States was when the Statue of Liberty was being installed in the 1920s. The government was short $125,000 of the money needed to finish the installation. So, through the radio and newspaper, the government asked the public to contribute funds. They asked for nickels, dimes, quarters, and any other small denomination. The appeal was successful.

Since then one of the most popular use of crowdfunding has been by independent brewers as they start up their beer breweries. Contribute a small amount, and you could get some of the first beer they produced.

In the case of the Statue of Liberty and beer production, the public is asked to contribute small amount of money. If the *crowd* liked the idea, the money was raised, but the people contributing were not involved in the operations of the business and not expecting a profit. They wanted to see the Statue completed and they wanted to get some good beer at a discount.

When the JOBS Act came along and introduced the word crowdfunding into the language of securities, it was adopted by anyone who was going to market their securities on the Internet.

In reality, today's crowdfunding Web sites are really just Internet marketing to accredited investors under Rule 506(c).

Regulation A offerings (Reg. A)

One of the other ways of raising money in a securities offering, without having a public offering, is Reg. A. The primary advantage of a Reg. A offering is that the group sponsor can market their securities using general solicitation and advertising, but is not restricted to only selling securities to accredited investors.

Previous rules, prior to the JOBS ACT

Reg. A was a seldom used option, (from 2012 to 2014 only 26 companies used Reg. A) allowing a sponsor to raise up to $5 million (expanded to $20 million in the JOBS ACT) in a twelve-month period from accredited investors, using full advertising and solicitation. Similar to a public offering, the registration requirements with the SEC and the application of Blue Sky Rules from the states made the time expended and the cost incurred to do a Reg. A offering impractical.

With the advent of Reg. D. Rule 506(c) which has no dollar limit, allows advertising, and restricts investors to being accredited, there was little need for Reg. A.

The JOBS ACT expanded Reg. A.

Part of the JOBS ACT was designed to open up capital markets to sponsors who wanted to raise larger amounts of money, employ advertising and solicitation, but not be hampered by the requirement of selling only to accredited investors. The JOBS ACT created a new part of Reg. A commonly referred to as Tier II or Reg. A +. Reg. A + allows group sponsors to raise up to $50 million in a twelve-month period, allows full use of advertising and solicitation, and opens up the sale of securities to non-accredited investors, and preempts the offering from the Blue Sky regulation of the states.

One of the main attractions of Reg. A+ is that a non-accredited investor is allowed to invest up to 10% of their annual income or net worth in each Reg. A+ offering they choose.

Only appears to be good for certain sponsors and offerings

There are problems with Reg. A+ that may limit its usefulness

First, these offerings are expensive. It is estimated that the cost of a Reg. A+ offering will be close to $100,000 plus the accounting fees and reporting fees.

Second, these offerings are time consuming. During the period of 2012 to 2014, it took the SEC an average of over 300 days to approve a Reg. A. offering. That time frame will not work for many real estate offerings.

Third, there are better alternatives, with the exception of the ability to attract unaccredited investors, Reg. D. Rule 506(c) gives a sponsor the ability to raise an unlimited amount of money, and the cost of the offering may be less than one half of a Reg. A+, and the offering can be on the street in a period of four to six weeks.

The SEC estimated that 95% of the Reg. D, Rule 506(c) offering conducted the year before Reg. A+ was approved could have used Reg. A+, but did not need to as it is cheaper and faster to stick to accredited investors and raise money through Reg. D, Rule 506(c).

Regulation of the Issuers

A second goal of the securities laws is to prohibit deceit, misrepresentations, and other fraud in the sale of securities.

Who is an issuer?

An issuer would be the person or persons who perform the actions that acquire control of the property and that cause the entity which will own the property to be formed.

There are four stages that are considered to be stages in which the issuer operates. During the *formation* stage, the issuer organizes the entity that will own the property. For most group sponsors, this would be a limited liability company or a tenant-in-common arrangement.

The acquisition of the property would be called the *acquisition* stage. Sometimes the formation and acquisition stage are lumped together and called the packaging stage.

The *management* phase involves managing the operations of the property and the entity.

The *disposition* phase involves the determination of when it is best to suggest to the investors the property be sold, marketing the property, managing the sale of the property, and the dissolution of the entity.

What are dealer activities?

Dealer activities involve the sale and distribution of the ownership interests in the entity that is being formed.

Unless the group sponsor has a relationship with a marketing group, it is likely the group sponsor will be considered the issuer and dealer in the same transaction.

The Securities Act of 1934 (Exchange Act)

This law is designed to protect the *masses* from *fraudulent actions of issuers and dealers of securities.* Under this law, the federal government must license all brokers and dealers of securities offered in the United States.

Most states allow the issuer to sell their own security interests. Most states state that no person may sell securities of another issuer and receive any payment as an incentive for their sale activity. People who sell security interests for remuneration need to be licensed as broker dealers or as agents of licensed broker dealers.

The Exchange Act regulates the issuance of licenses to people who act as brokers and dealers in securities sales.

Section 3(a)(4) of the Exchange Act defines the term *broker* as

> **IN GENERAL. The term "broker" means any person engaged in the business of effecting transactions in securities for the account of others, but does not include a bank.**

Section 15(a), provides that it shall be unlawful for any broker or dealer to effect any transaction in, or induce or attempt to induce the purchase or sale of any security, unless the broker or dealer is registered in accordance with Section 15 (b).

> **Securities Act of 1934, Section 15 -- Registration and Regulation of Brokers and Dealers**
>
> **15(a) Registration of all persons utilizing exchange facilities to effect transactions; exemptions**
>
> (1) **It shall be unlawful for any broker or dealer which is either a person other than a natural person or a natural person not associated with a broker or dealer which is a person other than a natural person (other than such a broker or dealer whose business is exclusively intrastate and who does not make use of any facility of a national securities exchange) to make use of the mails or any means or instrumentality of interstate commerce to effect any**

transactions in, or to induce or attempt to induce the purchase or sale of, any security (other than an exempted security or commercial paper, bankers' acceptances, or commercial bills) unless such broker or dealer is registered in accordance with subsection (b) of this section.

(2) **Manner of registration of brokers and dealers**

(3) **A broker or dealer may be registered by filing with the Commission an application for registration in such form and containing such information and documents concerning such broker or dealer and any persons associated with such broker or dealer as the Commission, by rule, may prescribe as necessary or appropriate in the public interest or for the protection of investors. Within forty-five days of the date of the filing of such application (or within such longer period as to which the applicant consents), the Commission shall--**

FINRA (Formerly the NASD)

The Exchange Act of 1933 allowed the establishment national securities associations. The Financial Industry Regulatory Association (FINRA) has been established to issue the licenses required under the Exchange Act and to regulate the behavior of those licensed to sell securities. Visit their Web site at www.finra.org

Generally, when the issuer is selling their own securities there is no need to have a securities license.

> *TIP: An analogy here is the "for sale by owner" situation in real estate. You can sell your own property without a real estate license, but you cannot sell someone else's property and you clearly cannot accept a commission without a real estate license. In the securities world, as an issuer, you can sell your own securities without a securities license, but you cannot sell someone else's securities and you can receive compensation related to the sale of a security.*

Because of the limited resources of the FINRA, it is impossible for it to license every issuer or dealer of securities offered in the United States and exemptions to the federal laws have been enacted.

The JOBS Act specifies that persons who conduct Rule 506(c) offerings, using general advertising or general solicitation will not, simply by virtue of this activity, be required to register as a broker or dealer under the Exchange Act, provided they must not receive transaction-based compensation, must not take possession of customer funds or securities, or must not be subject to disqualification under the Exchange Act.

Licenses that you would likely get

These are the licenses that you would normally obtain if you were going to be licensed to sell securities that are based on real estate.

Direct Participation Programs

A Direct Participation Program, called a DPP, is an investment where there is a flow through of tax consequences directly to the investor regardless of the structure of the legal entity. Sometimes the term *pass-through entity* is used to describe a DPP.

Examples of entities involved here would be limited partnerships, limited liability companies, and tenant-in-common interests. The underlying products could be real estate, cattle and horse breeding programs, oil and gas programs, and Subchapter S corporate offerings. In these investments, the investors report the income and losses on their tax return. This is different than in a corporation where the income and losses stay in the corporation and only dividends get distributed. The NASD has established two licenses for people who sell DPP programs.

Series 39

In the securities industry, the person who runs a brokerage firm is called a principal. Two principals are needed to run a securities brokerage firm. A person licensed as a Limited Principal-Direct Participation Programs would obtain a Series 39 license. Their firm could only sell securities in DPP programs.

Series 22

A person who wishes to work for principals in a DPP firm needs to have a Series 22 license and would be called a Limited Representative-Direct Participation Programs. The only securities that a Series 22 licensee can sell are those in DPP programs.

The relation between a Series 39 limited principal and a Series 22 limited representative is similar to the broker and salesman relationship found in the real estate industry.

Series 7

A person interested in selling securities that are not DPP programs would likely need to become a General Securities Representative and would obtain a Series 7 license and would work for a General Securities Principal.

Summary

In this chapter, you were exposed to the securities rules you need to be aware of if you are going to be a group sponsor. While not trying to make you a lawyer, this information is important for you to know in structuring your money-raising activities. This information may have been new to you as "It's a Whole New Business!"

Chapter Six: Income Tax and Accounting Issues

Sponsor's Duty

As a sponsor, you must, in effect, be the investor for your group. You must know how the tax law impacts the acquisition, operations, and disposition of the real estate your group owns. You must also know how the tax law impacts the operations of the entity you chose for your group.

As a fiduciary to your investors, you have a duty to perform your job as a prudent investor would and at the high level of performance the industry expects from people who take on the responsibility for the investments of others. It could be shown that ignorance of the tax law is either an intentional violation of a sponsor's duty or at the least a negligent violation of a duty owed to the investors. If nothing else, an understanding of what is presented here will equip the sponsor to ask relevant questions of the professionals the investment group will employ.

> *TIP: Often, brokers or agents say to me they do not need to know the tax law as "My clients don't ask me about taxes" or "My clients have accountants and attorneys who do that for them." It always amazes me that the agent does not want to learn this material for their own investments. Is it possible that the agents and brokers I meet do not file tax returns and pay taxes themselves?*
>
> *I believe that in performing the agency duties and fiduciary duties arising from being involved with deal-making activities, a real estate agent or broker should be familiar with the way the tax system impacts commercial and investment real estate. The knowledge in this section of the book will help you in your deal-making activities.*
>
> *In any event, as a fiduciary, you cannot use the "My clients don't ask me about taxes." and "My clients have accountants and attorneys who do that for them." answers. You must know the answers and be able to work with the accountants and attorneys employed by your group.*

Understanding the Tax Classification of Assets

Understanding the tax classification of assets is the starting point in working with sections of the tax law that will impact a group's investment performance.

Personal property vs. real property

As basic as it seems, the place to start in understanding the tax code is to know the difference between personal property and real property. We all are aware that the definition of real property starts with land. Everything that is not land or attached to land will be classified as personal property.

Experienced agents and brokers know the distinction is not as easy as it seems. For example, is carpeting classified as real property or personal property? The answer may depend on the method by which the carpeting is fastened to the floor. Are the awnings and bumpers attached to an industrial building at the loading dock area real property or personal property? It might surprise you that even though the bumpers are fastened to the building with sixteen-inch bolts the bumpers are considered personal property.

A group may own both real estate and some incidental personal property. The land bought and the buildings constructed on the land are considered real property. The buildings may contain articles of personal property. The evidence of ownership given to our investors, whether it is a certificate of interest in a limited partnership or a certificate of interest in a limited liability company, is personal property. The investment group owns real property, but the investors in the group own personal property.

Whether personal or real property, there are four different tax classifications for assets and each has a different tax treatment.

IRC Section 1221 Capital assets

Most assets that taxpayers own are classified as capital assets. However, some specific assets are not capital assets. IRC Section 1221 tells us that *all* assets are capital assets unless the asset is (1) a property which is a trade or business asset subject to depreciation, (2) real property used in a trade or business, or (3) inventory.

> **IRC Section 1221. Capital asset defined**
>
> **For the purposes of this subtitle, the term "*capital asset*" means property held by the taxpayer (whether or not connected with his trade or business) *but does not include-***
>
> (a) **stock in trade of the taxpayer or other property of a kind which would be properly included in the *inventory* of the taxpayer...**
>
> (b) **property used in his trade or business, of a character which is stock in trade of the taxpayer or other property of a kind *which is subject to the allowance for depreciation* as provided in Section 167, *or real property used in his trade or business* (emphasis added)**

127

Taxpayers may own assets used in their trades or businesses that are eligible for depreciation. They may own real property used in their trade or business. They may also own inventory which is held for sale to customers in the taxpayer's trade or business. Everything else they own is considered a capital asset.

Capital assets can be further broken down into two categories based on personal use or non-personal use.

An example of a personal use capital asset would be the personal residence of the taxpayer. An example of a non-personal use capital asset would be the ownership interest in a limited partnership that owns an apartment building.

A common example of a capital asset owned by an investment group would be raw land purchased with the intent of being held until the infrastructure is available for some other ownership entity to purchase and develop the land. This land is a capital asset in that it does not fall into the trade or business category and is not being offered for sale in parcels as an inventory item of a land developer.

When an investor or investment group owns Section 1221 assets, classified as capital assets, they may:
- Not take cost recovery
- Get long-term capital gain/loss treatment
- Get short-term capital gain/loss treatment
- Qualify for a Section 1031 tax deferred exchange
- Qualify for installment sale reporting

With the understanding of the tax treatment of raw land that is classified as a capital asset, we know the group may not take cost recovery but may qualify for long-term capital gains treatment when the group is ready to sell. As an alternative disposition strategy, the group may explore a Section 1031 exchange or an installment sale as ways to defer the taxable gain that will result from the land having appreciated in value.

IRC Section 1231 assets:

The second classification of assets contains a smaller number of taxpayer assets, but is the classification of assets most likely found in investment groups.

IRC Section 1231. Property used in the trade or business ...

(1) **General rule**

(2) **Definition of property used in trade or business**

(A) **General rule-** ... property *used in the trade or business*, **of a character which is subject to the allowance for depreciation provided for in Section 167,** *held for more than one year*, **and** *real property used in the trade or business, held for more than one year*, **which is not-**

(B) *stock in trade* **of the taxpayer or other property of a kind** *which would be properly included in the inventory* **of the taxpayer..., or**

(1) *property held by the taxpayer primarily for sale to customers* **in the ordinary course of his trade or business**

Section 1231 tells us that trade or business assets can be either personal property or real property.

Section 1231 personal property

Personal property used in the trade or business of an investment group that is held for more than one year is classified as a trade or business asset. If the asset was held for less than a year, it would retain its classification as a capital asset and, as we have seen, would not eligible for depreciation. It may actually be an expense item if it has a useful life of less than one year.

Common personal property assets owned by an investment group that would be classified as a Section 1231 asset would be the stoves, refrigerators, and air conditioning units that might be found in a furnished apartment or a hotel or motel.

Section 1231 real property

Real property, held for more than one year, and used in the trade or business of the investment group is classified as a trade or business asset.

Common real property assets owned by an investment group that would be classified as a Section 1231 asset would be an industrial building, an office building, a retail building, or a multifamily building or any of the other types of investment real estate.

Examples of undeveloped land owned by a group investment that could be considered Section 1231 assets would be a parking lot in a city, the land under a recreational mobile home park, or a working farm. All the parcels of land are being used in a trade or business, even though there may not be any buildings on the land.

Personal property or real property held as inventory in the business of an investment group is not classified as either a Section 1231 asset or a Section 1221 asset.

Section 1231 asset tax treatment

Trade or business assets have special tax treatment. If a group owns a Section 1231 asset, it:
- May take cost recovery
- May get long-term capital gain treatment
- May get Section 1232 net loss treatment
- May qualify for a Section 1031 tax deferred exchange
- Qualify for installment sale reporting

With the understanding of the tax treatment of trade or business assets, we know the group may strategize to take the maximum cost recovery deduction and may qualify for long-term capital gains treatment after a one-year holding period. When the group is ready to dispose of the property, alternative disposition strategies must be analyzed. As an alternative to an all cash sale, the sponsor may advise the group to explore a Section 1031 exchange or an installment sale as ways to defer the taxable gain, depending on whether their partnership agreement or operating agreement allows dispositions in any method other than a cash sale.

Inventory assets

Both Section 1221 and Section 1231 exclude assets that are determined to be held as inventory in the business of the investment group. Inventory assets are defined as those assets which are held by a taxpayer in their inventory and property held for sale to the customers in the normal course of their group's business.

IRC Section 1221 …. Does not include

(b) **stock in trade of the taxpayer or other property of a kind which would be properly** *included in the inventory of the taxpayer…*

IRC Section 1231 …. Does not include

(B) (1)

(A) **stock in trade of the taxpayer or other property of a kind which would be** *properly included in the inventory of the taxpayer…,*

(d) **property** *held by the taxpayer primarily for sale to customers in the ordinary course of his trade or business*

Tax treatment of inventory assets

Inventory assets have specific tax treatment. When investment groups are working with inventory assets, they may:

- Not take cost recovery
- Not get long-term capital gain/loss treatment
- Not get short-term capital gain/loss treatment
- Not qualify for a Section 1031 tax deferred exchange
- Not qualify for installment sale reporting

The decision to have an asset classified as inventory will come back to affect the investment group when the property is sold in that the tax deferral treatment under Section 1031 will not be available and all dispositions of inventory assets will be treated as cash sales and all income will be reported as ordinary income.

Here are some examples of real property owned by a group that would be considered inventory:

- A subdivision tract being sold by a group acting as a land developer or land sub-divider
- A shopping center being developed by the group for sale rather than for a long-term hold
- A distressed property purchased by an investment group with the intent of immediately selling the property after extensive remodeling and re-rental

Intent of owner

The facts reviewed in determining whether a property is inventory in the hands of the investment group can be confusing and have been the subject of many court cases. The issue with which the court is faced is: "What was the *intent* of the investment group toward the use of the property *at the acquisition* of the property?"

For example, if the investment group's intent when they bought the 15,000-square-foot lot on the corner was to build a small convenience center, get it rented, and immediately get it sold, it makes no difference that it took them several years to get the project completed, rented, and sold. Their intent was clearly to develop a property to hold as inventory to be sold to a customer, not to develop a property be held as a trade or business asset to be held for the production of income as a Section 1231 asset.

Regulations that have been issued regarding the above set of facts say that after the development of a property is completed, if the owner continues to hold the property and *operates it as a rental property for twenty-four months*, the income from the sale would not have to be considered income from a dealer activity, regardless of the original intent of the ownership group.

What if the investment group's intent upon purchasing the property was to develop a convenience center, get it rented, and hold the property for several years as a rental property, but just after the project was completed the group received and accepted a very attractive unsolicited offer on the property? The intent of the investor appears to have been to develop a rental property, which could be held for the production of income, clearly, a Section 1231 asset. It is incidental to the investor's intent the property was sold without there being a long-term holding period.

In both of the above facts, patterns of the investment group's intent upon acquisition of the asset will be the determining factor as to its tax treatment during the holding period and upon disposition.

It is not unreasonable to determine that a general partner or managing member could be considered to be negligent in their duties if they ignored the fact their group owns an asset that could be treated as inventory and failed to adequately document the original intent of the investment group toward the property. As a result of the negligence, the investors must report ordinary income and pay taxes on a transaction that was structured as a tax deferred exchange. The investors may not have any cash to pay the taxes, as all of the investors' equity was invested in the new property. The sponsor could be liable to the members of the group.

Summary of tax classification

The following is a summary of the tax treatment of the three classifications we have discussed.

Classification of Asset	Section 1231	Section 1221	Inventory
Cost recovery	yes	no	no
Capital gains	yes	yes	no
Tax deferred exchanges	yes	yes	no
Installment sale tax deferral	yes	yes	no

Accounting for Basis

The concept of basis in accounting has been developed to keep track of costs (i.e. cost basis). In addition, keeping track of our basis is important to assure that a dollar that has been taxed will not be taxed a second time. When a property sells, the sale price represents a return of the investor's cost basis adjusted for cost recovery and a payment of new dollars obtained by the investor. Only the new dollars get reported and are taxed at the appropriate tax rate.

Basis for tenant-in-common

This issue of accounting for basis in a tenant-in-common ownership only applies to the individual tenant-in-common interests. Each tenant is treated as owning a separate property interest. Each tenant will have their own basis. Some tenants-in-common may have a substitute basis as a result of having exchanged into their ownership position of the current property. Some investors will pay cash for their interest and establish their basis in a different manner. The sum total of all the individual basis accounts will not equal the cost of the property. We need not deal with the tenant-in-common basis calculations as they are the same as for an individual investor.

Basis in limited partnerships and limited liability companies

For more details on basis in limited partnerships and limited liability companies, see **IRS Publication 541** as it gives the rules of how basis and capital accounts are established and maintained in partnership accounting rules.

The concept of basis is applied at both the entity level and the individual investor level. The group will have a basis in the property and each investor will have a basis in their investment. The sum of the individual investors' basis will equal the basis of the group.

Acquisition of basis

Original basis for the investment group is the total cost of the property. It includes cash, loans acquired, and acquisition costs other than costs paid to a lender as prepaid interest.

Original Basis for the Group	
Cash Invested	
Plus:	Loans Acquired
Plus:	Acquisition Costs
Equals: Original Basis	

Original basis for the individual investor in a group investment is the total of the cash paid for the investment interest plus the portion of the debt that is allocated to the individual investor.

Original Basis for the Investor	
Cash Invested	
Plus:	Allocation of Loans Acquired
Equals: Original Basis	

The rule on the amount of loan allocated to an investor in a group investment is called the *at risk rule*. There are three possible outcomes of the at risk rule.

- If no one accepts personal liability, as in a non-recourse note, then no one is at risk and the entire loan gets allocated to the investors on a pro rata basis according to their ownership percentage.
- If all of the investors accept personal liability, as in a recourse note signed by each investor, then all are at risk and the entire loan gets allocated to the investors on a pro rata basis according to their ownership percentage.

- If some investors accept personal responsibility by signing for the loan and some investors do not sign, then the entire loan gets allocated to the investors who sign for personal liability on a pro rata basis.

Example of calculating the original basis for a group

For purposes of example, we will use the following assumptions relating to an investment in an income producing property owned by a limited liability company, managed by an individual managing member. The table shows the information on the acquisition of the property.

	Property Price	2,000,000
Less:	Loan Acquired	1,050,000
Plus:	Acquisition Costs	25,000
Equals:	**Cash Paid**	**975,000**

The original cost basis of the property is $2,025,000 calculated as follows.

	Cash Paid	975,000
Plus:	Loan Acquired	1,050,000
Equals:	**Original Property Basis**	**2,025,000**

In addition, the organizational costs of forming the group are $25,000. Organizational costs are a separate asset and have a separate basis of $25,000. The group will then have a total cost basis of $2,050,000 calculated as follows.

	Original Property Basis	2,025,000
Plus:	Organizational Costs	25,000
Equals: Original Group Basis		**2,050,000**

The total amount of cash that must be raised is $1 million, which is the total needed for the $975,000 cash down payment and the $25,000 organizational costs.

	Property Price	2,000,000
Less:	Loan Acquired	1,050,000
Plus:	Acquisition Costs	25,000
Equals:	Cash Paid	975,000
Plus:	Organizational Costs	25,000
Equals:	**Total Cash Needed**	**1,000,000**

Example of Member's Original Basis Calculation

For this example, we will assume the entity will raise the $1 million by offering 100 units, each priced at $10,000, with a minimum purchase of 10 units required by each investor. Two investors purchase all the units.

Member A will purchase 60 units for $600,000, 60% ownership.

Member B will purchase 40 units for $400,000, 40% ownership.

The managing member will make no cash investment and have no ownership.

The operating agreement calls for the members to be allocated profits, losses, and cash flow from operations on a pro rata basis, based on their percentage ownership as represented by the number of units owned by each member.

The $1,050,000 loan that was obtained by the limited liability company was a non-recourse loan, and as such, the loan will be allocated to each member on a pro rata basis, in relation to their ownership interests. 60% of the loan, $630,000, will be allocated to Member A, and 40% of the loan, $420,000, will be allocated to Member B. Their individual original basis accounts will be calculated as follows:

	Member A 60% Owner	Member B 40% Owner	Managing Member 0% Owner	Totals 100%
Cash Purchase of Units	600,000	400,000	0	1,000,000
Plus: Loan Allocation	630,000	420,000	0	1,050,000
Total Original Basis	1,230,000	820,000	0	2,050,000

The total of the two individual members' basis is $2,050,000, which is the same as the original basis for the investment group.

If the loan had not been non-recourse and both of the members signed, the allocation would be the same. If, however, only one of the members had signed on the loan and accepted personal liability, that investor would have received 100% of the loan as an allocation to their original basis.

As another option, suppose the managing member who invested no cash was the only signer on the loan, and accepted personal liability. In that case, 100% of the loan would be allocated to the managing member and none would be allocated to the other members.

In each of these possible outcomes, the total of the individual member's basis accounts will still equal the original basis of the entity.

Changes in basis

Basis changes in an investment group by accounting for the changes in basis in the property through the addition of capitalized entity items, the addition of capital additions to the property, and through the deduction for cost recovery and any partial sales of the property.

Adjusted basis for the property

Adjusted basis in the property can be calculated using the following formula.

	Original Basis
Plus:	Capital Additions
Less:	Cost Recovery
Less:	Partial Sales
Equals: Adjusted Basis in Property	

As the basis in the property changes, the appropriate term is to call the new number the adjusted basis.

For the purposes of our example, the real property purchased is classified as a Section 1231 trade or business property and, as such, qualifies for cost recovery. We will assume the available annual cost recovery deduction will be $40,000 and no other events will take place that impact our adjusted basis in the property. We will also assume a three-year hold on our entity.

Our adjusted basis in the property at the end of three years will be calculated as shown below.

	Original Basis	2,025,000
Plus:	Capital Additions	0
Less:	Cost Recovery	120,000
Less:	Partial Sales	0
Equals: Adjusted Basis in Property		**1,905,000**

Adjusted basis in the entity

Our total adjusted basis in the entity is the $1,905,000, which is the adjusted basis in the property plus the $25,000 of organizational costs, which, taking the most conservative approach for purposes of this example, will be written off at the termination of the entity.

	Adjusted Basis Property	1,905,000
Plus:	Organizational Costs	25,000
Equals: Adjusted Basis in Entity		**1,930,000**

Adjusted basis for individual members

The total of the individual adjusted basis for each investor will equal the total adjusted basis for the entity. The calculation at the end of three years of operation is calculated as follows.

	Investor A 60% Owner	Investor B 40% Owner	Managing Member	**Totals 100%**
Total Original Basis	1,230,000	820,000	0	**2,050,000**
Less: Cost Recovery	72,000	48,000	0	**120,000**
Total Adjusted Basis	**1,158,000**	**772,000**	**0**	**1,930,000**

The $120,000 cost recovery is allocated among the investors in a pro rata relationship as to their original basis.

The allocation of cost recovery on a pro rata relationship as to original basis is required as an adjustment to how the loan is allocated according to the at risk rules.

Using basis to calculate gain on sale and dissolution

The gain on the sale of the property will be calculated by subtracting the adjusted basis from the net sales price. The gain will be reduced by the capitalized Organizational Costs, as the entity will dissolve upon the sale of the property.

	Net Sales Price	
Less:	Adjusted Basis in Property	
Equals: Gain from Property		

Assuming a net sales price of $2,400,000, the gain on the sale of the property will be calculated as in the table below.

	Net Sales Price	2,400,000
Less:	Adjusted Basis in Property	1,905,000
Equals:	**Gain from Property**	**495,000**

Calculation of gain for the entity

Gain on the sale of the property and the termination of the limited liability company will be calculated as in the table below.

	Net Sales Price
Less:	Adjusted Basis: Property
Equals:	Gain from Property:
Less:	Organizational Costs
Equals:	**Gain on Dissolution**

We will assume the Net Sales Price of the property at the end of the three-year hold will be $2,400,000. The gain on the sale and dissolution of the entity will be as show in the table below.

	Net Sales Price	2,400,000
Less:	Adjusted Basis: Property	1,905,000
Equals:	Gain from Property	495,000
Less:	Organizational Costs	25,000
Equals:	**Gain on Dissolution**	**470,000**

Calculation of gain for the members

The operating agreement states that 100% of the gain or loss on the sale of the property will be allocated to the members in a pro rata relationship to their ownership percentages. The calculation of the sale price to be allocated to each member and the resulting gain to be reported by each member is as shown in the table below.

	Member A 60% Owner	Member B 40% Owner	Managing Member	Totals 100%
Net Sales Price	1,440,000	960,000	0	2,400,000
Less: Adjusted Basis in Property	1,143,000	762,000	0	1,905,000
Less: Organization Costs	15,000	10,000	0	25,000
Equals: Gain	**282,000**	**188,000**	**0**	**470,000**

Member A will be allocated 60% of the sale price. After subtracting their basis in the property and their share of the organizational costs, Member A would have $282,000 of gain.

Member B will be allocated 40% of the sales price. After subtracting their basis in the property and their share of the organizational cost, Member B would have $188,000 of gain.

While this example has demonstrated the use of basis for the entity and the members of the group, we have yet to determine the cash flows to each member on either a before tax or after tax basis. That is not the purpose of this section of the chapter.

Passive Loss Rule for Group Investors (IRC Section 469)

The *passive loss rule* has a direct impact on the area of group investments in commercial investment rental real estate in that it sets the way taxable income and losses are reported from the operations of rental real estate investments in general and, specifically, in limited partnerships and limited liability companies, regardless of the underlying investment. IRC Section 469 specifically identifies rental activities and limited partnership interests as coming under the passive loss rule. It is likely that interests in liability companies will also be deemed to be passive.

In a pass-through entity, such as a partnership or limited liability company, this rule is applied at the investor level in that the entity does not report income or loss but the investors will report their share of income or loss as a result of receiving a Schedule K-1 from the group.

Calculation of real estate taxable income (loss) from operations

First, we need to review the formula for real estate taxable income or (loss) from the annual operations of a property owned by a group.

	Net Operating Income
Less:	Deductible Interest
Less:	Cost Recovery Deductions
Less:	Amortization Deductions
Equals: Real Estate Taxable Income or (Loss)	

Real estate taxable income is reported during the tax year it is earned by the taxpayer. Increasing the total taxable income an investor reports from all activities increases the tax liability of the investor for that reporting period.

In the absence of the passive loss rule, real estate taxable losses when combined with taxable income from active or portfolio activities reduce the total taxable income an investor reports. Decreasing the total taxable income an investor reports decreases the tax liability of the investor for that reporting period.

What the passive loss rule does is establish rules regarding the timing of investor's ability to report real estate taxable losses and, as a result, establishes the timing of when the losses are available to the investor to shelter taxable income from other activities. All losses are eventually accounted for, but the passive loss rule establishes the timing of the recognition of the losses.

Statement of the passive loss rule
IRC Section 469

(c) **No losses from a passive activity may shelter active or portfolio income**

The rule states that taxable losses generated from the operations of an activity that is defined as a passive activity may not be used to shelter taxable income generated from an investor's active or portfolio income.

Activities that are covered by the rule

The following portion of Section 469 defines a *passive activity* as a trade or business in which the taxpayer does not materially participate. It also specifically identifies a rental activity as a passive activity.
IRC Section 469

(1) **Passive activity defined**

(A) **In general. - The term "passive activity" means any activity**

(2) **which involves the conduct of any trade or business, and**

(3) **in which the taxpayer does not materially participate**

(2) **Passive activity includes any rental activity**

141

Section (c) (1) (A) uses the term *"any trade or business."* Earlier we saw the Code defined a trade or business asset as a Section 1231 asset. We also determined that real property, owned by a group, is used in a trade or business and held for more than one year would be defined as a Section 1231 asset.

Section (c) (2) states specifically that rental activities are considered passive. Within the passive loss rule, *a rental activity is defined as an activity where the average rental period is more than seven days*. Most rental real estate properties, such as multi-family, retail, office, and industrial fall under this definition. Exceptions would be motels, hotels, bed and breakfast inns, and short-term health care facilities. These real estate investments are treated as operating businesses more than rental activities and are excluded from the passive loss rule. An investor who invests in a partnership or limited liability company that owns a hotel or motel may still be involved in a passive activity by the nature of their level of involvement in the management of the activity under Section (c) (1) (B) as explained below.

In subsection (c) (1) (B) the rule makes a distinction as to the level of involvement the taxpayer has in the operation of the trade or business by using the term *materially participate*. When the taxpayer does not materially participate in the trade or business, the taxpayer is determined to be involved in a passive activity.

This rule applies to taxpayers who individually own a property or taxpayers who own the property in a common enterprise where the taxpayer does not materially participate in the management of the activity, such as a limited partnership, a limited liability company, or general partnership.

As a result, the passive loss rule applies to most of the activities conducted by investment groups that own rental properties.

Investors who are covered by the rule
The followings portion of Section 469 tells us that this rule applies to individuals, estates, trusts, closely held C corporations, and personal service corporations who invest in a passive activity.

IRC Section 469-Passive activity losses and credits limited

(A) Persons described.- The following are described in this paragraph

(b) **any individual, estate or trust,**

(c) **any closely held C corporation, and**

(d) **any personal service corporation**

Material participation

Subsequent IRS regulations have established a two-part rule to determine when a taxpayer will not be covered by the passive loss rule by meeting the definition of being a material participant in a rental activity. The two-part rule requires a taxpayer to

spend a minimum of 750 hours per year in the operations of the rental real estate business; and

spend more than one-half of their total business time during the year on the operation of the rental real estate business.

If the taxpayer meets these requirements, the passive loss rules do not apply to them in that the law recognizes the taxpayer is really involved in running an active business. For the most part, investors in limited partnerships or limited liability companies will not meet this level of participation and will be subject to the passive loss rules.

Application of the passive loss rule during operations

An investment group that operates rental real estate is said to be conducting a passive activity. However, when the real estate is owned by a pass-through entity, such as a general partnership, limited partnership, or limited liability company, the entity does not report the taxable income or loss from operations as it is passed through to the individual investor. It is the individual investor in the group that is affected by the passive loss rule.

If the rental real estate produces taxable income, the investor will report that income along with taxable income from their active and portfolio activities. But if the rental real estate produces a taxable loss for the year the loss is not available to the investor to offset other taxable income.

Let's continue working with the example we used in the discussion of basis.

When the property was purchased, the building was rented. During the second half of year two, the tenant vacated and the building was empty for six months. A new tenant was obtained and received free rent for the first three months of the third year. The results for the three years of operations of the property are assumed to be as show in table below.

	Year 1	Year 2	Year 3
Net Operating Income	140,000	68,000	131,000
Less: Deductible Interest	80,000	78,000	76,000
Less: Cost Recovery Deductions	40,000	40,000	40,000
Less: Amortization Deductions	0	0	0
Equals: Real Estate Taxable Income or (Loss)	**20,000**	**(50,000)**	**15,000**

During the years of operations, the real estate taxable income (loss) from operation would be allocated to the members based on their percentage of ownership. Here is the record of the allocations on the Schedule K-1 for each of the three members in the group.

Member A 60%	Year 1	Year 2	Year 3
Real Estate Taxable Income or (Loss) Allocated	**12,000**	**(30,000)**	**9,000**

Member B 40%	Year 1	Year 2	Year 3
Real Estate Taxable Income or (Loss) Allocated	**8,000**	**(20,000)**	**6,000**

Managing Member 0%	Year 1	Year 2	Year 3
Real Estate Taxable Income or (Loss) Allocated	**0**	**0**	**0**

As can be seen, all of the real estate taxable income or (loss) is allocated to the members as none is allocated to the managing member.

Unused losses are suspended

The following part of the rule tells us the passive losses not used in one tax year will be available to the taxpayer in the next taxable year. The loss not used this year is in effect *suspended* until the next year. In effect, a suspended loss from one year is treated as occurring in the first day of the subsequent year.

> **IRC Section 469**
> 1. **Disallowed loss or credit carried to next year. -**
>   **Except as otherwise provided in this Section, any**
>   **loss or credit from an activity which is disallowed**
>   **under sub Section (a) shall be treated as a deduction**
>   **or credit allocable to such activity in the next**
>   **taxable year.**

There is a series of steps that an investor who has suspended losses will take to determine when the losses can be used. These steps, which must be followed in this order, are:

1. Passive losses can only offset passive income.
2. Losses not used this year are suspended until next year.
3. Suspended losses can be used to offset future passive income.
4. All suspended losses can be used on the sale of the activity that produced those losses.

The result of the application of the passive loss rule is not that the investor will lose the benefits of any taxable losses generated from the group investment. It is only the losses may not be used *currently*. Investors who invest in group investments producing taxable losses will be able to deduct these losses against income from other passive activities on an annual basis.

Here we will look at the taxable income or (loss) the members will report as a result of their real estate taxable income (loss) allocations and the application of the passive loss rule on operations. While this record keeping will not be done by the group but will be the responsibility of each member, a group sponsor should be aware of the process.

Member A 60%	Year 1	Year 2	Year 3
Real Estate Taxable Income or (Loss) Allocated	12,000	(30,000)	9,000
Passive Losses Suspended Beginning of Year (BOY)	0	0	(30,000)
Passive Losses Used	0	0	(9,000)
Passive Losses Suspended End of Year (EOY)	**0**	(30,000)	(21,000)
Ordinary Income Reported	**12,000**	**0**	**0**

In the first year, Member A will report $12,000 of ordinary income. In years two and three, there will be no income to report through the application of the passive loss rules. At the end of the third year, Member A has ($21,000) of suspended losses remaining.

We are assuming that this is the only passive activity the members have and the suspended losses are not used to shelter the passive income from other passive activities.

Member B 40%	Year 1	Year 2	Year 3
Real Estate Taxable Income or (Loss) Allocated	8,000	(20,000)	6,000
Passive Losses Suspended BOY	0	0	(20,000)
Passive Losses Used	0	0	(6,000)
Passive Losses Suspended EOY	0	(20,000)	(14,000)
Ordinary Income Reported	**8,000**	**0**	**0**

In the first year, Member B will report $8,000 of ordinary income. In years two and three, there will be no income to report through the application of the passive loss rules. At the end of the third year, Member B has ($14,000) of suspended losses remaining.

Managing Member 0%	Year 1	Year 2	Year 3
Real Estate Taxable Income or (Loss) Allocated	0	0	0
Passive Losses Suspended BOY	0	0	0
Passive Losses Used	0	0	0
Passive Losses Suspended EOY	0	0	0
Ordinary Income Reported	0	0	0

The managing member has no ordinary income to report as the operating agreement does not allocate income or (losses) to the managing member during the years of operations. The managing member has not accumulated any suspended passive losses.

Application of the passive loss rule at disposition of a passive activity

Upon the sale of rental real estate owned by a group investment, any suspended losses of the individual investors will be available to reduce the gain they must report as a result of the sale of the property.

IRC Section 469

(1) *Dispositions of entire interest* **in passive activity.—If during the taxable year a taxpayer disposes of his interest in any passive activity…the following rules shall apply:**

(A) **Fully taxable transaction.**

    (i) **In general.—If all** *gain or loss realized* **on such disposition is recognized, the** *excess of*

(I) *the sum of*

(ii) **any** *loss from such activity for such taxable year*

(iii) **any loss realized on such disposition, over**

• *net income or gain for such taxable year from all passive activities*

The above Section gives us the information to determine the correct order of the steps in which suspended losses must be handled when doing a fully taxable disposition of the entire interests in a rental property.

The following are the steps an investor in a group must follow on the sale of a passive activity:

- This year's operating losses on the passive activity which has been sold are used to reduce passive income generated from the sale of the activity by an unlimited amount even if the use of these losses creates a net loss at sale.
- Suspended losses generated by the passive activity, which have been sold, are used to reduce the passive income generated from the sale of the activity by an unlimited amount even if the use of these losses creates a net loss at sale.
- This year's operating losses on other passive activities are used to reduce the passive income generated from the sale of the passive activity to zero but no further.
- Suspended losses on other activities, which are not being sold, are used to reduce the passive income generated from the sale of the passive activity to zero but no further.

TIP: To understand the application of the passive loss rule on disposition, it is important that we view the sale as a sale of an activity, not a property, because the investor in the group does not own the property. The income generated on the sale must be treated as passive income. This passive income is treated along with all other passive income or passive losses in the activities of the investor for that year.

Calculation of Gain to Be Reported after the Application of Suspend Losses

	Member A 60% Owner	Member B 40% Owner	Managing Member	Totals 100%
Net Sales Price	1,440,000	960,000		2,400,000
Less: Adjusted Basis Property	1,143,000	762,000	0	1,905,000
Less: Organizational Costs	15,000	12,000	0	25,000
Equals: Gain	282,000	188,000	0	470,000
Less: Suspended Losses	(21,000)	(14,000)	0	
Equals: Reportable Gain	**261,000**	**174,000**	**0**	**N/A**

In this example, both Member A and Member B will apply their suspended losses at the time they have a complete disposition of the activity. The suspended losses reduce the gain they report on the investment.

The passive loss rule did not limit the members' right to take a deduction for the operational losses of the property. What the passive loss rule did is adjust the timing of when the losses are deductible and, in this case, the losses offset income from this passive activity but not other active or portfolio activity income the members may have had.

On the members' tax return the gain will be allocated between cost recovery recapture and long-term capital gain.

Miscellaneous provisions

In the case of an investment group that owns multiple properties, each property is treated as a separate activity. The managing member must be able to work with the group's CPA to be certain that each property is tracked as a separate activity. The result of each activity is reported separately in the annual reports provided to the individual members.

This process gets extremely complicated when a member has a diversified investment portfolio and has invested in multiple passive activities. Each activity must be tracked separately by the investor's CPA. The managing member has no duty to be part of this accounting for the individual group member.

The rules on the treatment of suspended losses when the activity is sold in an installment sale or disposed through a tax deferred exchange are more complicated and should be discussed with a tax attorney or CPA.

Even at this point, the member does not know if they actually have a gain to report. The gain from the disposition of the activity may be just one of several capital transactions the member has during the tax year. Some transactions will result in gains and some will result in losses. Some transactions will be short-term and some will be long-term. All capital asset transactions are netted together to determine the end results of the member's tax year. The process of netting capital gains and losses from multiple capital asset dispositions is a topic for another book.

Capital Accounts

In addition to accounting for the entity's basis and the individual investor's basis, federal tax law requires the maintenance of an individual capital account for each investor. The group sponsor has a duty to review the work of the entity's CPA to be certain the capital accounts are being maintained as required in the operating agreement or partnership agreement. This is a totally new area for many agents and brokers who concentrate on deal-making activities because capital accounts are only required in group investments. There are several types of capital accounts present in group investments, but this section will deal with the capital account maintained in accordance with IRC Section 704 (b) as this is likely to be the capital account called for in the operating agreement or partnership agreement.

The following discussion is designed to give the real estate group sponsor a basic familiarity with the operations of a capital account so the group sponsor can converse with the group's CPA and answer basic questions from investors.

Capital accounts reflect the economic equity of the investor

In general, an investor's capital account reflects the equity or the economic interest the investor has in the entity.

If an investor has a positive balance in their capital account, it usually indicates the proceeds the investor will receive if their interest is liquidated.

If an investor has a negative balance in their capital account, it may indicate the partner will have to make an additional contribution to the entity if their interest is liquidated.

If an investor has more than one interest in a group, such as a general partner who also owns limited partnership interests, one capital account will be maintained to include all interests.

Events that cause a capital account to increase

Here is a list of the most common events that will cause a capital account to increase.

- The amount of money contributed to the entity by the investor
- The fair market value of property contributed to the entity by the investor, net of any encumbrances assumed by the entity as a result of the contribution
- The distributive share of the entity's income and gain allocated to the investor

Events that cause a capital account to decrease

Here is a list of the most common events that will cause a capital account to decrease.

- The amount of money distributed by the entity to the investor
- The fair market value of property distributed by the entity to the investor, net of any encumbrances assumed by the investor as a result of the distribution
- The distributive share of the entity's losses and deductions allocated to the investor
- The distributive share of the entity's syndication and organizational costs

Example of capital account maintenance for the entity

Continuing with our example, we have everything we need to calculate the capital account balance of the entity except for the cash distributed. Here are additional assumptions regarding cash distributions.

The members agreed to retain positive cash flow until there was $100,000 in reserves. As a result, they were able to handle the negative cash flow caused by the tenant vacating the property. At no time was there a sufficient cash balance to allow distributions to the members. The $84,000 retained from the cash flow from operations was distributed at the dissolution of the limited liability company.

Here is a chart showing the annual cash flows from operations of the property.

	Year 1	Year 2	Year 3	**Total**
Net Operating Income	140,000	68,000	131,000	**339,000**
Less: Annual Debt Service	85,000	85,000	85,000	**255,000**
Equals: Cash Flow	**55,000**	**(17,000)**	**46,000**	**84,000**

The property sold for a net sales price of $2,400,000, and the outstanding mortgage balance had been reduced to $1,029,000 from $1,050,000. The sales proceeds were $1,371,000 according to the following calculation.

Net Sales Price	2,400,000
Less: Mortgage Balance	1,029,000
Equals: Sales Proceeds	**1,371,000**

Using the results of the acquisition, operation, and disposition of the property and the dissolution of the limited liability company, we can trace the capital account balance for the limited liability company as follows.

Event in Limited Liability Company	Change in Capital Account	**Capital Account Balance**
Initial Capital Account Balance		**0**
Cash Contribution from Members A	600,000	**600,000**
Cash Contribution from Member B	400,000	**1,000,000**
Year 1: Real Estate Taxable Income	20,000	**1,020,000**
Year 2: Real Estate Taxable (Loss)	(50,000)	**970,000**
Year 3: Real Estate Taxable Income	15,000	**985,000**
Sale: Distribution of Gain	495,000	**1,480,000**
Dissolution: Organizational Costs	(25,000)	**1,455,000**
Dissolution: Distribution of Cash Generated from Operations	(84,000)	**1,371,000**
Dissolution: Distribution of Cash Generated from Sale of Property	(1,371,000)	**0**

The capital account for the entity started at zero and ended at zero.

Example of capital account maintenance for individual members

With the information from the sample property and sample limited liability company, we can see the calculations needed to maintain the capital account of each of the three members. Each individual capital account starts at zero and must end at zero.

As an additional assumption at the sale, the managing member is allocated 10% of the net sales proceeds.

Event in Limited Liability Company	Member A	Member B	Managing Member	Totals
Initial Capital Account Balance	0	0	0	**0**
Cash Contribution	600,000	400,000	0	**1,000,000**
Year 1: Real Estate Taxable Income	12,000	8,000	0	**20,000**
Year 2: Real Estate Taxable (Loss)	(30,000)	(20,000)	0	**(50,000)**
Year 3: Real Estate Taxable Income	9,000	6,000	0	**15,000**
Sale: Distribution of Gain	297,000	198,000	0	**495,000**
Dissolution: Organizational Costs	(15,000)	(10,000)	0	**(25,000)**
Dissolution: Distribution of Cash Generated from Operations	(50,400)	(33,600)	0	**(84,000)**
Dissolution: Distribution of Cash Generated from Sale of Property	(740,340)	(493,560)	(137,100)	**(1,371,000)**
Adjusting Entry	(82,260)	(54,840)	137,100	**0**
Ending Capital Account Balance	**0**	**0**	**0**	**0**

The operating agreement calls for the managing member to be allocated 10% of the net sales proceeds, which equals $137,100. The allocation gives the managing member a negative capital account of ($137,100). All capital accounts start at zero and end at zero. Therefore, there must be an adjusting entry of income or gain to increase the managing member's capital account to zero. This $137,100 will be reported as income by the managing member. Since the managing member never acquired any basis in the entity, this amount will be reported as ordinary income. The $137,100 is really a fee for providing services and will be treated as ordinary income.

Since $137,100 of the gain must be reallocated to the managing member, Member A and Member B will have a capital account adjustment, reducing the amount of gain they receive by their pro rata share of the $137,100. This adjusting entry will reduce the gains the members report.

Phantom income

Phantom income is a term that is heard when an investor in a group receives a distribution of taxable income but does not receive any cash with which the investor could pay the tax.

Most commonly, you will hear investors complain about phantom income in the situation of a foreclosure. When the lender reacquires the property and the entity is dissolved, all the capital accounts must be adjusted to a zero balance. Generally, the investors have negative capital accounts at the time of this event. The adjustment needed to increase a capital account is a distribution of taxable income.

The result in this situation is the investor has a large taxable income to report but the property is gone and the entity has no cash to distribute. Here is an example. The adjusting entry amount of $800,000 must be reported and the appropriate tax must be paid. However, as a result of the foreclosure, the investor receives no cash distribution from which the tax can be paid.

Capital Accounting at Foreclosure	
Mortgage Foreclosed	800,000
Capital Account Balance	(800,000)
Adjusting Entry	**800,000**

Summary

In this chapter you saw information from the tax code and some accounting issues that you are probably not dealing with every day. You'll need to get up to speed on these, so that you at least have a working knowledge of them when you sponsor a group since this is required of you as "It's a Whole New Business!"

Chapter Seven: Private Placement Memorandum (PPM)

If a sponsor determines that what they are going to be offering to potential investors will be considered a security, a disclosure document, commonly referred to as a Private Placement Memorandum (PPM), will have to be prepared and delivered to each investor before their investment is made in the entity. An attorney with experience in the securities industry must be used to prepare these documents. To draft these documents yourself would likely be considered the unauthorized practice of law, which is a misdemeanor in many jurisdictions. The purpose of the PPM is to provide the full disclosure envisioned in the federal securities laws. This section will cover the basic construction of a PPM as outlined in **Guide 5** most recently revised and issued by the **Securities and Exchange Commission. Release No. 33-6405 (June 3, 1982) (47 FR 25140).** While adherence to Guide 5 is required in public offerings, most securities attorneys follow Guide 5 when drafting a PPM.

TIP: The PPM is a very important document but can sometimes be imposing and at times you will feel like no one is reading it and they are making their investment decisions only based on what you say. You really need to get the potential investor to read it. One sponsor puts a handwritten note on the cover of each of his PPMs that says something like this, "Here is the PPM. It is very important that you read this from cover to cover. Call me if you have any questions as to what it says."

Basic disclosures

A detailed PPM is your insurance policy in the event charges of violations of the disclosure requirements of the security laws, as discussed in the chapter on security laws, are invoked by an investor. The information provided should be complete. The group sponsor should always be prepared to provide information on the basis of full disclosure.

Summary of offering

The cover page of the document should include a brief summary of the offering, the termination of the offering period, the minimum investment required of an investor, a brief statement of significant risks involved, and other pertinent information, such as:

- The name, address, and telephone number of the sponsor and the names of persons making investments for the group
- The intended termination date of the group
- Whether the sponsor and its affiliates will receive substantial fees and profits in connection with the offering

- The amount of time from formation of the group that the investor might have to wait to receive distributions
- The properties to be purchased. If a substantial portion of the proceeds are not committed to specific properties, that fact must be stated.
- Description of depreciation method to be used
- Statement of the maximum leverage to be used by the group as a whole and on individual properties

Suitability standards for the investors in the group

A statement of the standards to be utilized in determining the acceptance of investors into the group should be included. In addition, a statement as to what actions the sponsor will follow to assure adherence to the suitability standards established.

There should be a discussion of the importance of the suitability standards, i.e., the investment may be illiquid, the tax benefits may only be of value to an investor in a particular tax bracket, and there is the possibility of adverse tax consequences if an investor completes a sale of the interests in the group prior to the completion of the investment contemplated by the group.

Summary of the use of proceeds

The sponsor must include a tabular summary showing the use of proceeds which contains estimates of offering expenses, amount available for investment, non-recurring initial investment fees, prepaid items and financing fees. Amounts paid to the sponsor should be disclosed. Amounts should be disclosed in both dollar figures and in percentage figures.

	EXAMPLE OF SUMMARY OF THE USE OF PROCEEDS SECTION				
	Estimated Application of Proceeds of this Offering				
		Minimum		Maximum	
		Dollar		Dollar	
		Amount	Percent	Amount	Percent
Gross Offering Proceeds		$	100.00%	$	100.00%
Offering Expenses:					
Underwriting Expenses					
Organizational Expenses and Acquisition Fees		$_____	____%	$_____	____%
Amount Available for Investment		$_____	____%	$_____	____%
Prepaid Items Related to					
Purchase of Property					
Cash Down Payment					
Working Capital Reserves		_____	_____	_____	_____
Proceeds Invested					
Amount Available for Investment		_____	_____	_____	_____
Total Application of Proceeds		$_____	____%	$_____	____%

The Sponsor and its affiliates may receive a maximum of $ _____ (____ %) if the minimum dollar amount is sold and $ _____ (___ %) if the maximum dollar amount is sold from the sellers of the property as real estate commission on the purchase of the property(ies). Real estate commissions are generally paid by the seller of the property rather than the buyer. However, the price of a property will generally be adjusted upward to take into account this obligation of the seller so than in effect the group will bear a portion or all of the commission on the purchase price of the property. The group also expects to pay a commission on the sale of the property(ies) which will reduce the net proceeds to the group.

Compensation and fees to the sponsor and affiliates

In a tabular form, the sponsor should include a summary, itemized by category, of all compensation, fees, profits and other benefits which the sponsor or affiliates of the sponsor may earn or receive in connection with the offering or operation of the group.

This summary should show whether the compensation relates to the offering and organization stage, the development or acquisition stage, the operational stage or the termination stage of the group. Maximum fees to be paid during the first year of the operation of the group should be shown, assuming that maximum funds are raised.

If any compensation is based on a formula, the formula should be explained and illustrated. If compensation to the sponsor is based on a given return to the investors in the group, it should be stated whether the return is cumulative or non-cumulative.

Conflicts of interest

In order to provide full disclosure an investor would need to make an informed decision, the PPM must contain a complete listing of conflicts of interest that might be present during the acquisition, operation, and disposition stages of the property. The sponsor must disclose conflicts, such as the following:

- If the sponsor has groups engaged in similar investments
- If the sponsor has the authority to invest funds of this group in other groups in which the sponsor has an interest
- If the sponsor has an interest in the property or properties in any other investment in which this group will be investing
- If the sponsor has an interest in properties adjacent to the property or properties this group will be acquiring
- If the sponsor acts as a real estate broker, mortgage lender or property manager for other group investments in which the sponsor has an interest, even if not as a sponsor
- If the compensation plan for the sponsor may create a conflict between the interests of the sponsor and the interests of the group
- If the sponsor has the right to sell or lease property to a group in which the sponsor has an interest
- If the sponsor has the right to purchase property from the group without a vote from the group
- If the sponsor can find a replacement sponsor without the consent of the members of the group

- If the sponsor can receive any insurance brokerage fees or other fees related to the property without consent of the group

Fiduciary responsibilities of the sponsor

A full discussion of the fiduciary duties owed by the sponsor to the group and its members should be included. Guide 5 suggests the following statement, outlining a broad definition of the duties of a fiduciary, be included in a limited partnership PPM, and it would likely be wise to include a modified version of it in a PPM for a limited liability company.

A General Partner is accountable to a limited partnership as a fiduciary and consequently must exercise good faith and integrity in handling partnership affairs. This is a rapidly developing and changing area of law and Limited Partners who have questions concerning the duties of the General Partner should consult with their counsel.

A PPM should list the typical rights, authority, power, responsibilities, and duties of the group sponsor. A sample list of what would be included would include the rights to do the following:

- To acquire, develop, hold, and dispose of property
- To borrow money and, if needed, mortgage the property
- To place the title of property to be recorded in the name of the group
- To purchase insurance on behalf of the group
- To employ persons in the operation and management of the property
- To prepare or cause to be prepared the reports as required by the group legal document
- To open accounts so as to deposit funds in banks and savings and loans
- To choose the tax year of the group
- To raise equity for the group
- To amend the legal agreements of the group
- To purchase equity units for their own account
- To conduct an exchange of equity units for real property

Risk factors

A list of the various risks that an investor may face if they choose to invest in the group should be discussed so the investor has the information needed to make an informed decision. Typical risk factors could include the following:

- Whether or not the group has obtained an IRS ruling as to the tax status of the group
- Whether or not there is a possibility the tax liability in any year will exceed the cash distribution in corresponding years and, as a result, the payment of taxes will be an out of pocket expense
- Whether or not on a sale of one or all of the properties the tax liability may exceed the cash distribution at the sale
- Whether or not the risk that an audit of the group's records will trigger an audit of the individual investors' tax records
- Whether or not any of the group's objectives, such as high leverage, increase the risk associated with the investment
- Whether or not the risk that no market for the individual units in the group exists and the investment is illiquid in the event the investor desires to liquidate their interest
- Whether or not there is a risk associated with the possibility the Federal or State income tax laws may change effecting the results of the investment

Many offering circulars use the same boilerplate risk disclosures over and over, but what is really needed is a full discussion of the risks in *this* investment. What happens if the anchor tenant moves out of *this* property or if the construction of *this* property gets delayed six months? Generally, you can talk about general risk issues, but what is really needed is a discussion of what happens if these issues arise in this investment.

Prior performance of the sponsor

Various reports of the results of prior investment groups sponsored by the current group sponsor are required to give the investors the information they need to make an informed decision about whether they want to invest with the sponsor.

Narrative report of all groups sponsored in the last ten years

Guide 5 requires that a narrative report of the track record of the prior performance of the real estate investment groups that have been sponsored by this sponsor during the past ten years in similar investments should be included. The narrative should include the following information:

- Number of programs sponsored
- Total amount of money raised from all investors
- Total number of investors
- Number of properties purchased by sponsor
- Aggregate dollar amount of properties purchased
- Percentage of properties by property type, i.e. retail, office, industrial, or apartments
- Percentage of properties by new construction or existing properties
- Number of properties sold

Prior performance in raising and investing funds in completed offerings

Guide 5 states that a prior performance table, in substantial conformity with the following example, must be included to report the sponsor's experience in raising and investing funds where the money raising has been completed.

	Program 1	Program 2
PRIOR PERFORMANCE TABLE		
Experience in Raising and Investing Funds		
Dollar amount offered $		
All figures expressed as Percentages		
Dollar amount raised		
Less offering expenses:		
Organizational expenses:		
Other expenses:		
Reserves		
Percent available for investment:		
Acquisition costs:		
Prepaid items and fees related to purchase of the property:		
Cash down payment:		
Acquisition fees:		
Other fees:		
Total acquisition cost:		
Percentage leverage:		
Date offering began:		
Length of offering (in months):		
Months to invest 90% of amount available for investment:		

Operating results of prior programs that have been completed

Guide 5 states that a report showing operating results of prior programs, in substantial conformity with the following example, must be included to report the sponsor's experience in similar offerings that have been completed, or have *gone full cycle*.

Operating Results of Prior Programs			
	Program 1		
	Year 1	Year 2	Year 3
Gross Revenues			
Profit on sale of property			
Less: operating expenses			
Interest expense			
Depreciation			
Net Income			
Taxable Income			
from operations			
from gain on sale			
Cash generated from operations			
Cash generated from sales			
Cash generated from refinancing			
Cash generated from operations,			
sales, and refinancing			
Less: cash distributions			
from operating cash flow			
from sales and refinancing			
from other			
Cash generated (deficiency) after cash distribution			
cash distribution			
Less: special items			
Cash generated (deficiency) after cash distributions			
and special items			
Tax and Distribution Data per $1,000 Invested			
Federal Income Tax Results			
Ordinary income (loss)			
from operations			
from recapture			
Capital gain (loss)			
Cash Distributions to Investors			
Source			
Sales			
Refinancing			
Operations			
Other			

Compensation to sponsor in past groups

A prior performance table in substantial conformity with the following example must be included to report the compensation paid to the sponsor in past group investments.

PRIOR PERFORMANCE TABLE		
Compensation to Sponsor		
	Program 1	Program 2
Date offering commenced		
Dollar amount raised		
Amount paid to Sponsor from offering		
Underwriting fees		
Acquisition fees		
real estate commissions		
advisory fees		
Other		
Other		
Dollar amount of cash generated from operations before deducting payments to sponsors		
Amount paid to sponsor		
from operations		
Property management fees		
Group management fees		
Reimbursements		
Leasing commissions		
Dollar amount of property sales and refinancing before deducting payments to sponsors		
cash		
notes		
Amount paid to sponsor from property		
sales and refinancing:		
Real estate commissions		
Incentive fees		
Other		

Performance results of completed programs

A prior performance table in substantial conformity with the following example must be included to report the results of the sponsor's programs that have been completed.

```
┌─────────────────────────────────────────────────────────┐
│              Results of Completed Programs                │
│                                                           │
│  Group Name                                               │
│     Dollar Amount Raised                                  │
│     Number of Properties Purchased                        │
│     Date of Closing of Offering                           │
│     Date of First Sale of Property                        │
│     Date of Final Sale of Property                        │
│  Tax and Distribution Data per $1,000 Invested            │
│     Federal Income Tax Results                            │
│        Ordinary Income (loss)                             │
│           from operations                                 │
│           from recapture                                  │
│     Capital Gain (loss)                                   │
│     Deferred Gain                                         │
│        Capital                                            │
│     Ordinary                                              │
│  Cash Distribution to Investors                           │
│        Sales                                              │
│        Refinancing                                        │
│     Operations                                            │
│        Other                                              │
│  Receivable on Net Purchase Money Financing               │
└─────────────────────────────────────────────────────────┘
```

Management

A complete description of the people involved in the management of the group or the properties.

Investment objectives and policies

A description of the nature of the property intended to be purchased and the criteria to be utilized in evaluating proposed investments and whether or not the group investment will be a semi-specified or blind pool investment.

Description of real estate purchased

A description of the property or properties that will be purchased by the group should be included. If there is a property that within a reasonable probability will be purchased by the group, there should be a complete description.

Federal income taxes

The PPM should include a discussion of the significant federal and state income tax implications of the proposed investment. If there is a reason to get any advance letter rulings or tax opinion letters, these disclosures should be included in the offering material.

Summary of group management document

A brief summary of the material provisions of the agreement used to manage the group. The group management agreement may be the limited partnership agreement or the operating agreement if a limited liability company.

Reports to group members

A description of all reports and other documents that will be furnished to the members of the group as required of the management document. A complete schedule for the distribution of the reports to the group members should be included.

Distribution plan

A description of the plan as to how the investment units will be sold should be included.

Sometime the offering is a mini-max offering where the program needs to raise a minimum amount before it can invest the proceeds. After the minimum amount is raised, the sponsor continues to raise money up to the maximum amount stated in the private placement memorandum. This is common in a construction project or a semi-specified offering where more than one property is anticipated to be purchased.

Rule 10b-9 of the Exchange Act requires that a mini-max offering must provide that investor funds will be returned if the required minimum proceeds are not raised by the stated offering deadline. Courts and this Commission repeatedly have stressed the importance of this requirement, which gives investors assurance the offering will go forward only if enough investors demonstrate by their purchases the risk associated with the offering is worth taking and the price being paid for the securities is fair.

Each investor is comforted by the knowledge that unless his judgment to take the risk is shared by enough others to sell out the issue his money will be returned.

The Legal Agreement

The legal agreement that will govern the manner in which the group will be run must be included in the PPM. This would be either the limited partnership agreement, in the case of a limited partnership, or the operating agreement of a limited liability company. The legal agreement will include information about the following issues:

- Formation of the group
- Investment of the members of the group
- Accounting rules the group will follow
- Management plan of the group
- Rights of the members of the group
- The ability to assign or transfer an ownership unit in the group investment
- Termination of the group
- Other provisions

Subscription Agreement and Offeree Questionnaire

The Subscription Agreement is an application document signed by the investor. The investor subscribes to purchase a certain number of investment units in the group being formed. Often, the check for the purchase from the investor is attached to the Subscription Agreement.

The Offeree Questionnaire is a questionnaire the investor completes to help the sponsor assess the suitability of the investment for that particular investor in matching the investor with the suitability requirements of the investment group.

Investment Analysis

There should be a complete analysis of the investment. The property should be analyzed. The extra cash needed to be raised for working capital and the fees charged because it is a group investment must be included in an analysis of the entity.

Results should be reported in total and on a per unit basis. A sample is shown in the chapter on investment analysis.

Summary

In this chapter, we looked at what should be included in a PPM that your attorney will prepare for you when you are going to raise equity from investors. Much of this information may look new to you, but then "It's a Whole New Business!"

Chapter Eight: How a Group Sponsor Makes Money

Here Is a Picture of the Syndication Business Using T-Bars

	Property	- Debt	- Sponsor	= Investors
0	(Price)	- (Loan)	- (Sponsor Risk)	= ($$/Units)
1	CFBT	- ADS	- Fees/%s	= Cash Dist.
2				
n	SPBT	- Payoff	- Fees/%s	= Cash Dist.
			PV = @ ?%	IRR

THE SYNDICATION BUSINESS

In an earlier chapter, I discussed the business of being a syndicator from the aspect of the risk-reward relationship. I said that the investors put in the money and expect returns. The sponsor does not put in any money but assumes the risks. Then I suggested that the way the sponsor determines if they want to do the syndication is to take a present value (PV) approach to the fees or percentage cash distributions they will receive through the operation and disposition phases of the syndication. It was suggested that for a stabilized property the discount rate used to determine the present value of the sponsor's position is around 15%. On a value-add or for a construction project, the discount rate should be increased to 25%.

So now we turn to a discussion of what fees and percentage distributions are standard in the syndication industry. In reality, there are as many combinations of fees and distribution percentages as there are transactions as the particular deal structure will determine what will work. For example, some projects do not offer cash for distribution during the holding period, but rather, all the money is made on the sale. Other projects, like a fund that lends money, primarily provide cash for distribution during the operations. But I can talk about common arrangements encountered when drafting offering documents for syndicators.

Below, you can see a list of typical sources of revenues available to the sponsor.

Sources of Revenue for you*

- Acquisition Fees
- Ownership Interests
- Asset Management Fees
- Disposition Fees
- Share of Operational Cash Flows
- Share of Refinancing Proceeds
- Share of Sales Process

*Possible Real Estate Fees for Licensees

Acquisition fees

An acquisition fee is a fee the sponsor receives at the formation stage of the offering. The fee compensates the sponsor for time, effort, and expertise used in obtaining the investment opportunity. Most often the acquisition fee is expressed as a percentage of the money invested in the offering. Typical fees range from 5% to 10% of the money raised. Sometimes, the acquisition fee is stated as a percentage of the price of the property acquired when there is a specific property. Generally, this method uses 2% to 5% of the price of the property.

Ownership interests

Often the sponsor takes a direct ownership interest in the offering as a form of compensation for bringing the investment opportunity to the market. The investors put up all the money for a percentage of the company and the sponsor gets the balance. Typical ownership interest splits at formation range from 30% to 50% for the sponsor. Taking ownership interests directly at formation can cause a tax problem for the sponsor because if the ownership interest has an immediate ascertainable value, it is treated as ordinary income and is taxable when received.

Asset management fees

The sponsor should receive payment for managing the company, apart from managing the real estate which they may not actually do. The asset management fee is an expense allocated to the company, not to the property. Asset management fees are sometimes calculated as a percentage of the revenue the company produces, usually 1% to 2%., paid on a quarterly basis. In other situations the asset management fee is based on the amount of money raised from investors. If the company raised $2 million dollars, the asset management fee might be 1% to 2% of that amount, paid annually. Finally, many sponsors set the amount of the asset management fee as a fixed annual dollar amount, paid monthly or quarterly.

TIP: I recommend that every sponsor take an asset management fee that is not based on the amount of cash that can be distributed from the operations of the company. There will come a time where the sponsor may decide not to distribute any cash. Having a management fee will allow the sponsor to continue to get paid for the work they do on behalf of the company.

In addition to the three fees mentioned above, the sponsor will likely receive a percentage of the cash available to distribute from the operations of the company.

Share of operational cash flows

When the company generates cash flow that can be distributed, it is common that the sponsor shares in the cash flows. Frequently, the sponsor will receive between 25% and 50% of the cash flows generated by the operations of the company.

Share of refinancing proceeds

When a property is a value add or a new construction project there can be a time when the property can be refinanced to return the investors a portion of their original cash investment without selling the property. If the sponsor has ownership interests in the company, they may get a share of the refinancing proceeds.

In addition, the sponsor may get a percentage of the refinancing proceeds. It is common for the refinancing proceeds to go directly to the investors *as a return of capital.* If the proceeds exceed the investors' original investment, the sponsor and the investors will split any excess. Sometimes the refinancing proceeds are simply split between the investors and the sponsor without regard to whether the sponsor has any ownership interests.

Share of sales proceeds

When the sponsor has an ownership interest, the sales proceeds are split on a pro rata basis. But when the sponsor is only sharing in the cash distribution, it is likely that the investors will get a distribution of sales proceeds to equal a return of their original investment, as a priority distribution. Then the balance of the cash available for distribution is split between the investors and the sponsor. It is common for the sponsor's split to be between 30% and 50%.

Real estate commissions for deal-making activities

Sometimes the sponsor, who is a real estate licensee, will collect commission on the sale of the property. But as explained earlier, doing a syndication just for real estate commission is a poor decision on the sponsor's part, and any cash earned from a commission should not be considered when calculating the present value of the sponsor's position.

WATERFALL (Suggested)

Operations

- Pay interest to Manager on loans made to Property LLC, if any
- Repay Manager for loans made to Property LLC, if any
- Pay arrearages in preferred return, if any
- Pay current preferred return, if any
- Distribute available cash flow from operations according to splits specified in Operating Agreement

Capital Transactions

- Return of capital from sale or refinance
- Fees to Sponsor specified in Operating Agreement
- Distribute available cash according to splits specified in Operating Agreement

While there are endless variations on how cash is distributed in a syndication, the most common pattern of distribution, called a waterfall, is as described in the graphic above.

Waterfall from operations (returns on capital.)

The first two steps are designed to pay the manager back for any dollars owed to the sponsor and any interest due on those amounts for the time the sponsor has left their money in the transaction.

171

Once the manager is paid back, any cash available for distribution is used to make up any arrearages in the preferred return and the current preferred return that should be paid to the investors.

Once the manager and the preferred returns are dealt with, any remaining cash available for distribution is split according to the percentage split included in the operating agreement.

Waterfall from a capital transaction (return of capital)

When there is a return of capital, generally as a result of a refinance or sale, it is common for the investors to get a priority return up to the amount of their original investment. Then any fees due to the sponsor are paid. Remaining cash available for distribution is then split according to the percentages found in the operating agreement.

SPONSOR COMPENSATION PLANS

- 50% Ownership
- 50% of Profits
- 25% Profits + Management Fees
- 20% CFs + Management Fees
- 4%, then 30%, after 100% return

- 35%, no preferred return
- 35% after 12% preferred return
- 10% Ownership + 50% CFs after 10% preferred return
- *Normal fees for services provided*

The graphic above shows some typical compensation plans that have been written in recent operating agreements I have reviewed.

50% ownership

Some offerings call for the sponsor to immediately get 50% ownership of the company. For example, if a company pays $2 million for a piece of land on an all-cash purchase, the company owns the land, but the investors may only own 50% of the company and the sponsor owns the other 50%. In this case, the $1 million of ownership the sponsor obtains is taxable as ordinary income as it is an amount earned by the sponsor. The tax is due, but the sponsor never really receives any cash with which to pay the tax.

The bad news is that the income is taxable, but the good news is that the sponsor will establish a basis in their ownership position and may be able to claim capital gains treatment in the future.

50% of profits

As an alternative to taking ownership and having the taxable ordinary income result, the sponsor could take 50% of the profits, subordinated to the investors getting a return of their investment. Since there is no ascertainable value associated with the future profits, there is no taxable income at the point of formation of the company, but all income received in the future will be treated as ordinary income.

In this case, the good news is that there is no taxable income at the formation of the company, but any income earned in the future will be ordinary income. An analysis, by a CPA would be needed to see which of these two alternatives will provide maximum benefit to the sponsor.

25% of the profits + management fees

In this plan, the sponsor takes management fees throughout the operations and then at the sale takes 25% of the profits, subordinated to the investors receiving a return of their investment.

20% of the cash flows + management fees

In this situation, all cash flows available for distribution are split with the investors getting 80% and the sponsor getting 20% from both operations and capital events. In addition, the sponsor will receive management fees.

4% then 30% after a 100% return

This cash distribution plan was used in a development project involving several buildings to be built for sale. There was not going to be any cash available for distribution from operations as all cash would be coming from the sale of the buildings. The sales proceeds would be split with the investor receiving 96% and the sponsor getting 4% until the investors received a complete return of their investment. After that event, the split would go to 70% for the investors and 30% for the sponsor.

35%, no preferred return

Many experienced syndicators find that the more uncomplicated the cash distribution plan is the more the investors understand it, and that understanding helps in the marketing efforts. In this offering, the sponsor created a simple 65% split in favor of the investors with 35% going to the sponsor.

35%, after a 12% preferred return

It is very common for a sponsor to structure an offering so that the investors get a return before the sponsor gets anything. This is called a preferred return. In this case, the investors were going to get a return of 12% annually, based on the amount of capital they had invested, and any remaining cash available for distribution would be split with investors getting 65% and the sponsor getting 35%.

TIP: As an observation, I have found that as the preferred return goes up, the split the sponsor takes also goes up. For example, if the preferred return is 4% the split to the sponsor may be 30%. If the preferred return is 8%, the split to the sponsor might be as high as 50%. If the investors get paid well first, the sponsor can take a larger split of what cash is remaining available for distribution.

10% ownership + 50% cash flows after 10% preferred return

Sometimes, the compensation structure gets more complicated. In this structure, the sponsor will take immediate ownership of 10% of the interests in the company and then take 50% of the cash available for distribution after the investors have received a 10% preferred return.

Normal fees for services provided

This plan is not recommended. Do not take on the risk of being a sponsor if all you are going to receive are fees for your deal-making activities. Let someone else take the risk!

TIP: As can be seen there are many ways that a sponsor can make money through a syndication. This is not a charity! There are risks involved, and you should be paid for taking on the risks. In reality, you are the one making the investment work and you should get paid. Without sponsors who are willing to take the risks, many investors will not get to invest in real estate. You provide a service. Get paid! But do not make the distribution plan so complicated that the potential investors do not understand it. If they do not understand it, they will not buy!

Summary

In this chapter, we have discussed some of the ways a group sponsor can make money that are different than you may have seen in other real estate transactions when you act only as a deal maker., Remember, there is a risk/reward issue in this business. Make sure you structure your syndication so that you get rewarded for the risks you take, because "It's a Whole New Business!"

Chapter Nine: Forming and Operating Your Next Group Investment

These are the Steps to Take in Forming and Operating Your Next Group Investment

Choose a Limited Liability Company

Today, the most popular choice of entity that sponsors are choosing is the limited liability company. Investors have heard that the limited liability company is the entity of choice if they are interested in having input into the daily management of the property. Sponsors are choosing the limited liability company as the entity of choice so they can take advantage of the limited liability offered the group sponsor, as opposed to the unlimited liability faced by general partners in general partnerships or limited partnerships.

There are two possible reasons that a limited partnership could be the entity of choice, instead of a limited liability company. First, in a small group of financially sophisticated investors who are expected to make large cash investments, the sponsor might want shield them from the possibility of the issue of fiduciary duty present among members of a limited liability company. By making them limited partners without any management responsibility, it would be very difficult for a claim of breach of fiduciary duty to be made against any of the partners.

The second possible reason for choosing a limited partnership as the legal entity in which to form your group would be if the number of investors you expect to have gets large enough that a stronger central management function is needed. You can create a strong central management function in a limited liability company through the operating agreement, but the operating agreement is always subject to modification more easily than a limited partnership agreement.

Establish an Entity to Act as Managing Member

The first action you should take is to form a limited liability company for you to use as the managing member of the second limited liability company you will form to actually own the property you will operate. You can use this managing member LLC to form each of your limited liability companies you form in subsequent group sponsor offerings.

We will call your limited liability company Managing Member, LLC.

Protects your assets

In the event of legal action against a sponsor, it is important to limit the assets of the sponsor that will be vulnerable to legal attack. If the sponsor is an individual and a civil action is commenced, every asset of the sponsor is at risk. If the sponsor is married, all of the assets of the community are at risk. By having Managing Member, LLC act as sponsor, only the assets within that limited liability company are vulnerable. Some sponsors will form a separate limited liability company to act as sponsor of *each* investment group they form.

While that may be the most prudent way to conduct the business of being a group sponsor, it is likely the number of groups you will sponsor will be small enough that one managing member entity will be sufficient. At some level of volume, perhaps a second entity to serve as managing member will be appropriate.

Allows for flexibility

By having Managing Member, LLC with its own operating agreement act as sponsor, transactions relating to the investment can be handled more simply than if the sponsor were required to include a spouse or if the sponsor were required to comply with corporation regulations in making decisions and executing legal documents.

Allows for continuity

One question an individual, acting as a sponsor, will encounter is "What happens to the investment if something happens to you?" Sponsors have lives and deaths, bankruptcies, divorces, and health problems. Managing Member, LLC will have a legal life separate from the individual sponsor. Having at least two members in Managing Member, LLC will give potential investors more assurance in your management plan. The investors who have invested with the sponsor do not need the additional risk of unexpectedly having an investment without an ongoing management function as would be likely to happen with a single person limited liability company or with an individual sponsor.

Form the Limited Liability Company that Will Own the Investment

Once Managing Member, LLC is formed, you should form the limited liability company that will sell investment interests and will own the property. A limited liability company can be formed in many states with one member, and Managing Member, LLC can be that member.

Let's call our limited liability company Operating, LLC.

With Operating, LLC formed, bank accounts can be opened to accept investment funds from investors. Offers can be written on properties in the name of Operating, LLC, so that no assignment issues will arise and no disclosures will have to be made about markups or hidden profits.

Operating, LLC, once formed, can operate according to the terms of the operating agreement and can conduct all the business activities needed to complete admission of investors and to complete the property acquisition.

Choose a Specific Property

It will be easier for you to successfully form and fund your next group if you choose to go to the investment marketplace with a specified offering that is designed to own one specific property.

As you develop a track record of performance in group investing, you will be more successful in fund-raising, and then doing a semi-specified offering with more than one property will be possible. It is possible that you will never do a blind pool real estate private placement offering, but you might.

Choose a property type based on your experience

A specific offering has an identified property or several identified properties that will be acquired and managed by the Operating, LLC. Raising money is easiest for this form of investment group. Only after the sponsor develops a track record in setting up, operating and dissolving investment groups can the sponsor expect to be successful in raising investor money for semi-specified or public investment programs where one or more properties are specifically identified but extra money is raised to purchase additional unspecified properties.

By choosing a product type in which you have experience, the investors will face fewer risks, the property management should be more effective, and raising money will be facilitated.

Referring to the IDEAL acronym from Chapter Two, each property type provides specific benefits for the investors. For example, a single tenant, net leased property will generate income from rent payments, equity build-up from debt repayment and can be purchased using leverage. Investors looking for spendable income and equity build up through principal reduction would invest in this type of investment.

Investors who are looking for rapid appreciation and tax shelter through depreciation but are not interested in current spendable income would not be interested in this type of investment.

When you choose the specific property type in which you will operate, i.e., industrial, office, multifamily, or retail, you will have a very good idea of where your investors will be found based on the benefits the property produces.

Choose a specific group of investors and concentrate on their goals

Another way of choosing a specific property type would be to determine what benefits your group of investors would most likely want. For example, perhaps you already have identified a group of potential investors who are not interested in current income but want appreciation, tax benefits through cost recovery, and the advantages of leverage. They may well want to invest in multifamily properties. Another group of investors who are primarily interested in equity build-up may be interested in development projects or value added investments.

When a specific group of investors is identified as the target for raising money, their investment goals can be identified. There is a specific property type that will produce the exact benefits the investors need.

Number of investors and amount of the raise

Many sponsors plan to keep the equity they plan to raise to less than $2,500,000 and the number of investor to less than ten. Many sponsors want to be sure that each investor in the investor group can contribute a minimum of $50,000.

Provide for positive cash flow

Currently, with the exception of development projects, investors expect current cash flow distribution, on at least a quarterly basis. The management plan for Operating, LLC should be designed so the first cash distribution will occur within the first six months after the acquisition of the property.

It is not important that the early cash distribution be the full amount expected to be achieved as the property operations mature during its ownership. For example, if the property were expected to produce a 6% annual distribution, it might be acceptable to distribute 2% during the first year, especially if the management plan calls for the retention of cash flow to build up reserves or complete needed capital improvements.

Secure the property

You must, in some way, secure the specific property or properties to be purchased by Operating, LLC. Without securing the property you will find it very difficult to raise investor funds. If Operating, LLC raises a large portion of the investment funds needed to purchase the property but not 100% and must return the funds to the investors, it will be very difficult to raise money for your next group. Be sure that you have a plan to close on the property you have identified yourself, regardless of the amount of money you actually raise.

The surest way to secure the property is for Managing Member, LLC to have the funds needed to purchase the property and contribute it to Operating, LLC. Operating, LLC would have to have a provision in the operating agreement that allows it to repay Managing Member, LLC the amount of equity that was used to purchase the property.

Barring your ability to totally front the capital needed to purchase the property, there are several other ways to secure a property. All of these have been successful in certain situations.

Enter into a binding purchase agreement

Operating, LLC could identify the property or properties to be purchased and put them under contract. You would write the offer in the name of Operating, LLC. The seller would not have to worry about any rights to assign your interest, which may raise concerns as to whether you have the ability to perform.

Whether or not a contingency clause regarding the group's ability to raise the money to close is a viable clause will largely depend on the current state of the market in which you are attempting to purchase a property. In some markets, if a closing cannot take place in thirty days, the sellers are unwilling to tie up their property. Some markets would see a six-month closing as lightning fast!

Generally, this strategy is accomplished through the use of leverage from a traditional lending source that will provide short-term financing to facilitate the purchase of the property.

Obtain an option

Operating, LLC may be able to place a property under option with the ability to exercise the option at some time in the future. Some investment groups have used this acquisition strategy to facilitate the purchase of the property at a specified price upon reaching a specified level of fund-raising. While the fund-raising is progressing, the seller has the right to continue to market the property.

Contribute a property owned by a member of the group

Perhaps one of the members of Managing Member, LLC has a property that would be a good property to put in your next investment group, even if only to syndicate a portion of the equity. Perhaps a person who might not be a member of Managing Member, LLC but would like to be a member of Operating, LLC has a property that would be a good property for your first group.

I have seen this happen several times and the strength of this approach is there is already an operating history for the property. As projections are made as to the future operations, the projections will likely be met, which creates confidence in your investors and builds a strong track record for you. Additionally, the property is already under control so the potential investors are not concerned about the sponsor's ability to close the acquisition of the property.

Prepare the Private Placement Memorandum (PPM)

The Private Placement Memorandum (PPM) contains three major sections; the basic disclosures, the legal agreement, and the subscription agreement and offering questionnaire. See the complete discussion of the PPM in the chapter that covers them.

Use an attorney to draft and review any documents you intend to use for your group investment. Choose an attorney who will be available to you to be involved with all the operational aspects of your group.

Use a CPA to review the financial analysis of the property or properties your group intends to acquire and any track record history you intend to include in your offering material. Choose a CPA that will be available to you to be involved with all the operational aspects of your group. The CPA will be used annually at a minimum to review the annual report to the investors and prepare the annual tax returns for both federal and state reporting.

Basic disclosures

This is a partial list of the items to be dealt with in the PPM.
- The name, address, and telephone number of the sponsor of the group
- The formation date and intended termination date of the group
- Whether the sponsor and/or the sponsor's affiliates will receive substantial fees and profits in connection with this offering
- The amount of time from formation of the group the investor might have to wait to receive distributions
- The description of the property or properties to be purchased
- The description of the depreciation method to be used
- A statement of the maximum leverage to be used by the group
- A statement of the suitability standards for investors in the group
- A table explaining the sources and uses of proceeds

- Explanation of the compensation to the sponsor and affiliates of the sponsor
- A listing and explanation of the conflicts of interest between the sponsor, its affiliates, and the group
- The fiduciary responsibilities of the sponsor on behalf of the group
- The risk factors relating to an investment in the group
- Tables showing the prior performance of the sponsor in other similar group investments
- A management plan for the property
- An explanation of investment objectives and policies the sponsor will use to manage the group
- A description of the real estate being purchased or a business plan if it is a blind pool
- An explanation of the impact of federal income taxes on an investment in the group
- An explanation of significant federal income tax implications of the operations of the property
- A summary of the important components of the Operating Agreement
- A plan as to when and how the sponsor will provide reports to the group members
- The explanation of how the units in the group will be distribution to investors

Operating agreement

As you are using a limited liability company, you will be using an operating agreement which will contain the following major sections.

Formation, Name, Purpose, Definitions
- The agreement should state the authority under which the group is organized, such as the state limited liability law.
- The intent of the members as to how the group will be run i.e., a corporation or partnership should be stated.
- The agreement should state the official name of the group and address of the place of business for the group.
- The nature of the business of the group should be spelled out. Does the group plan to operate an apartment building or does the group intend to build and sell an office building?
- The term of the life of the group should be stated.
- The agreement should state the name and address of the agent for service of process for the group so that official documents may be delivered to the group.

Capitalization of the group

- A statement of what the expected total capital amount raised from the investors and the timing of the capital contribution should be included.
- If there is a staged pay-in arrangement, there should be a statement of what happens if an investor does not complete the investment.

Rights and duties of the manager

- The managing member of the group should be identified.
- A statement of the ability of the managing member to make major decisions for the group, such as acquiring property, selling or disposing of property, encumbering property, admitting additional members, and conducting banking transactions should be included.
- If the managing member has the authority to enter into contracts with affiliates, employ others, or delegate duties to unrelated parties, the ways this will be handled should be stated.
- If the managing member is to contribute property or funds to the group, the amounts and methods of contribution and reimbursement should be stated.
- Methods for accepting a resignation or affecting the removal of the managing member and methods for choosing the replacement for the managing member should be stated.

Compensation: Reimbursement of expenses

- The methods and amount of compensation to the managing member should be set forth in the operating agreement. If the managing member is expected to pay for expenses of the group, the method of reimbursement should be established.
- There are endless ways to formulate the compensation a sponsor may receive in a group investment, and there is a separate section on this at the end of this chapter.

Rights and obligation of the members

- The operating agreement should contain a statement regarding the limitation of liability for the members according to the applicable laws.
- There should be a statement that the members may be provided with a list of all the members of the group upon certain conditions.
- Many states require that some percentage of the members must approve the sale or encumbrance of the property. The operating agreement should state the law or a more restrictive rule under which the group members have chosen to run their group.
- A statement as to the circumstances under which the members may have access to and examine the books of the group should be included. The location of the books and records of the group should be identified.

Meetings of the members

- If meetings of the members are anticipated, whether they are to be annual or at some other frequency, the place of the meetings, the method of noticing the meetings, and what constitutes a quorum should be stated.
- If there is a provision for proxies in lieu of attendance at these meetings, the policies should be stated.

Capital contributions, capital accounts, advances

- A definition of capital accounting that includes the establishment of capital accounts, how they change, and the actions taken at the termination of the group with regards to the investors' capital accounts.
- A statement to the effect that treasury regulations may change during the life of the group and capital accounting methods may change.

Division of profits and losses

- A statement of the method under which the members and managing member will divide the profits and losses of the group should be set forth in detail.
- A statement that explains when and if special allocations of cash distributions and taxable income and losses will be allowed should be included.

Distributions

- The frequency and method of making distributions to the group members and the managing member should be explained.
- A statement as to whether all distributions are to be in cash, or possibly in the form of equity in property should be made. Usually, all distributions are to be made in cash.
- A statement of whether the group will be reporting on a fiscal year or calendar year basis should be included.
- A statement as to where the banking relations for the group will be conducted should be included.
- The projected time frame for the distribution of financial statements to the members should be included.
- It should be stated whether the managing member may make decisions regarding the tax matters for the group.

Additional members

A statement should be included regarding the possible addition of additional members after the original members have been admitted.

Transfers of the ownership of an investment unit

- There should be a statement of the method by which the ownership of investment units may be transferred.
- A statement of how substituted members and their membership interests will be treated, if it will be any different the treatment of the original members should also be included.

Right of first refusal to transfer ownership interest

- Sometimes, the transfer of investment units is not a voluntary matter. Death, divorce, and bankruptcy happen, and the investment unit must be transferred or liquidated.
- It should be stated as to whether the managing member or other group members may have a first right to purchase the investment units before a unit may be sold to a person who would become a new member of the group.
- If an appraisal of the investment unit is required in an involuntary transfer, the appraisal process should be spelled out.

Dispute resolution

The agreement should state the method by which disputes among the members of the group will be resolved. If a specific arbitration arrangement is anticipated, it should be spelled out in detail.

Dissolution and termination of the group

- The events that will cause an automatic termination of the group should be described.
- The method in which an election to terminate the group may be held should be stated.
- Procedures as to the events of winding up of the group should be enumerated.

Miscellaneous provisions

Generally, this section contains the information regarding the addresses of where notices are to be sent to the various parties to the operating agreement.

Exhibit A: The Property

In a specific offering, a complete property package or investment summary should be included.

Exhibit B: Operating Agreement

The operating agreement to be used to run the company must be provided to each investor.

Exhibit C: Subscription Agreement

The subscription agreement is simply an application document signed by the potential purchaser of investment units.

- The subscription agreement should contain information about the number of units the investor would like to purchase and the total dollar amount of the investment to be made.
- The subscription agreement should contain information about the suitability standards that will be applied to the investor who would like to purchase investment units in the group.
- The subscription agreement should contain information regarding the process of accepting the potential investor's money, where it will be deposited, and when it will be deposited. The investor's check should be attached to the subscription agreement.
- The subscription agreement should recite the suitability standards the sponsor will use to make a decision as to whether the investor will be accepted into the group.

Exhibit D: Offeree questionnaire

The offeree questionnaire is a questionnaire the potential investor will be asked to complete to help the sponsor determine if the investment is suitable for the potential investor.

- The offeree questionnaire will help the sponsor determine if the investor meets the standards to be considered accredited or will be considered non-accredited.
- The questionnaire will ask about the potential investor's previous investment experience with group investments.
- The questionnaire will ask about the potential investor's annual income for the last two or three years. It may be reasonable to ask the potential investor to attach the first two pages from the previous two federal income tax returns. This will help the sponsor establish the veracity of the potential investor's statements regarding their income.
- The questionnaire will ask about the potential investor's net worth. It may be reasonable to ask the investor to submit a financial statement. This will help the sponsor establish the veracity of the potential investor's statements regarding their assets.
- The questionnaire will ask the potential investors about the amount of investment that will be made in this investment group. This information should be checked against the information on the subscription agreement.

Market the Investment Units

Generally, the next group investment you will do will truly be a private placement, where you probably know most of the potential investors before you identify the property or start raising the funds.

Remember the material about general solicitation in the chapter covering federal securities laws. No advertising or general solicitation is allowed. A list of traditional sources of investors is included in the following list:

- Current clients of yours
- Past clients of yours
- Referrals from past clients
- Business acquaintances
- Current property owners
- Referrals from your attorney or accountant
- Other real estate licensees
- Referrals from other real estate licensees
- Acquaintances from investment classes, seminars and other professional meetings
- Relatives

Manage the Entity

It is advisable to spell out, in some detail, the method in which you plan to communicate with your investors. The plan becomes a road map for you, and the investors will count on you following this plan. Do not commit to any of these events unless you intend to follow through with them.

Communication

The operating agreement will specify the minimal level of communications the sponsor must have with the members of the group. It will also set forth the time line for these communications and the form in which the communication will be conducted.

It is advisable to communicate at least quarterly with the members of your group. More frequent reporting may be important if major events are taking place in the investment.

Some group sponsors schedule an annual meeting of the investors where all investors get together to vote on important business decisions regarding the investment. In most states, there is no requirement of an annual meeting of the group members.

An annual communication that includes the income tax information and an annual report on the operations of the property will be due in the first quarter of each year.

Fiscal responsibilities

The sponsor of the group is held to the highest degree of fiduciary duty to the group and the members of the group.

Annual income tax reporting

The group needs to file a federal income tax return each year. The return is an informational return only as Operating, LLC is a pass-through entity. The informational report, federal Form 1065, reports the results of the group as one entity. A Schedule K-1 is prepared for each group member, reflecting their share of the operational result of the group, according to the profit sharing arrangement described in the operating agreement. A copy of all Schedule K-1s is attached to the informational report. Every group member must be provided a copy of their individual Schedule K-1.

Operating, LLC may need to file a state income tax return, also, which is also of an informational nature. In certain states, there is a minimum annual tax due as a result of operating under the limited liability company rules of the state.

It is possible that Operating, LLC may have to file with the county some annual statement. It is also possible the county has levied some sort of tax on the income received by the group, even if that income is in the nature of rental income.

While there is no date set for the distribution of annual tax information to the group members, the group sponsor should be aware that investors expect to receive this information by February 15, as they receive their W-2 and 1099 forms around that time. Delaying the distribution of the annual tax information to the group members will likely result in a number of telephone calls to the sponsor and some disgruntled investors, as they cannot file their return and get their refund until they have the information from the group. Being late with the distribution of these materials will show the group members the sponsor lacks organizational skills.

Closing Out the Group

The steps listed below are typically the steps, in order, that are required when the group dissolves.

Pay liabilities

All of the bills of the group need to be paid and some reserve for undiscovered bills must be considered. An estimate and reserve for potential federal and state income tax preparation and reporting fees may need to be established.

Pay investors

> The members should be paid according to the rules as spelled out in the operating agreement for the group.

Pay the sponsor

> The sponsor should be paid according to the rules as spelled out in the operating agreement for the group.

File final tax return

> The final returns for both the federal and state income taxes must be filed and any taxes due must be paid. The final tax return will be marked as a final return to identify it as such to the various organizations that collect taxes. Informational returns must be provided to the members.

File dissolution documents

> Appropriate dissolution documents must be filed. States who regulate the legal entity chosen by the group may have specific documents that must be filed to notify the state the entity is no longer doing business within the state.

Abandon fictitious name report

> File the correct report within the county or counties of the state in which the group was organized and approved to do business so the county knows that Operating, LLC is no longer in operation.

Compensation to the Sponsor

As stated earlier, there are many ways to formulate compensation to the sponsor during the operations of the group investment. Here is a discussion of the most common methods.

Fees at formation

> A sponsor of the group can be entitled to collect real estate commissions generated on the purchase of the property or properties acquired to the entity. However, these fees are the traditional deal-making fees we discussed in the beginning of the book and should not be considered when calculating the present value of the sponsor's position in the offering.
>
> Other fees generated at the formation of the group could be organizational fees or consulting fees that could be called for in the operating agreement. An initial management fee could be paid to the sponsor for services provided during the formation of the group. Activities performed could be supervising the initial

operations of the property, including all aspects of tenant lease negotiations and operating expenses, establishing and implementing an accounting system for the group and installing the computer system on which the group will keep their books and provide the required reports to the members of the group.

The operating agreement should spell out whether the sponsor will be reimbursed for any expenses advanced on behalf of investment group during the formation period.

Ownership interests

In certain entities, the IRS requires the sponsor of the group to have at least a 1% ownership in the entity. Regardless, the manner in which the sponsor acquires ownership interests in the investment group will have tax implications for the sponsor.

Ownership interests granted up front

If the sponsor is simply granted an ownership interest and that interest has an ascertainable value, the receipt of the interest by the sponsor is a taxable event. The sponsor will have to report the receipt of the value of the interest and pay taxes on the value of the interest at ordinary rates. Through the payment of the taxes, the sponsor does establish a basis and monies received in the future should be reportable as capital gains.

For example, assume that an investor invests $1 million for the purchase of a piece of land, on a free and clear basis in a limited liability company with one member and one managing member. The managing member has rezoning ability and immediately receives a 20% of the ownership interests in the limited liability company at formation.

The way the IRS looks at this situation for the sponsor, is that at the start of the day the sponsor did not have any ownership interests in this entity on their balance sheet. At the end of the day the sponsor had an ownership interest worth $200,000 (20% of $1 million free and clear land). That is earned income of $200,000 which is reportable and subject to ordinary income tax rates. The reporting of the income and subsequent payment of taxes establishes a $200,000 basis for the sponsor. If the property is classified as a Section 1221 asset which is not inventory, and the 20% ownership grows in value, the increase will be reported as capital gain, subject to favorable tax treatment.

Ownership interests are subordinate to future event

There is another way the sponsor can receive ownership benefits through sponsoring a group. The sponsor can receive benefits subject to some other event happening. In this way, the benefits are subordinate to some other event happening and have no value at the time they are awarded. The sponsor may never receive anything and, as such, there will be no taxable income to report upon the formation of the group. When, and if, the sponsor receives any benefits, they will be reported as ordinary income.

For example, if, in the same fact pattern as above, the investor invests $1 million but retains 100% ownership interests in the entity, the operating agreement could grant to the sponsor a distribution of 20% of the cash proceeds from the sale of the property, *subordinated to* the return to the investor of their original investment.

The way the IRS looks at this arrangement is the sponsor receives nothing of current ascertainable value and does not have a taxable event. The sponsor does not establish any basis in this subordinated interest. If the sponsor receives any cash proceeds, they will be treated as a fee for services and will be reported as ordinary income.

Fees during operation

The operating agreement may state the sponsor may be entitled to receive property management fees related to the management of the property or properties owned by the entity. In addition, the sponsor could be allowed to receive real estate brokerage fees for leasing activities related to the property during the operation of the property. These are fees that result from deal-making activities and should not be considered by the sponsor when calculating the present value of assuming the risks of being the sponsor of this group.

The sponsor may be entitled to receive fees as a result of the activities undertaken to manage the entity itself. These fees can be set as a flat fee, as a percentage of effective income, or a percentage of the value of the asset owned by the group.

The operating agreement should state if the sponsor is entitled to be reimbursed for expenses paid on behalf of the entity involved in managing the property and properties and the entity itself.

Fees at disposition

The sponsor may be entitled to collect a commission on the sale of the property or properties owned by the entity based on the compensation plan outlined in the operating agreement. This is a deal-making fee and should not be considered by the sponsor when calculating the present value of assuming the risks of being the sponsor of this group.

The sponsor, in lieu of a commission on disposition, may be entitled to a flat fee, regardless of who provides the deal-making activities resulting in a sale.

The sponsor would also be entitled to whatever benefits are attached to the ownership interests it owns or future distributions acquired by the sponsor, as discussed above.

Summary

Now that you have seen the steps that I recommend for you in forming and operating your next group, be sure to review the sample PPMs of other sponsors or interview attorneys and see if they will let you review some of the documents they have prepared. The documents you must prepare for a group investment are different than what you have done for a transaction with an individual investor, but then "It's a Whole New Business!"

Final Words

As I worked on this edition of this book, I tried to include a discussion of the questions and comments I receive through emails, phone calls, or when I make live presentations on group investments. There is so much a group sponsor needs to know that it cannot be included in one book. If you are interested in learning more, I might advise you to attend one of our live workshops or take our video course that accompanies this book at www.exceedce.com.

While researching material to include in this book, it became apparent to me that as soon as this third edition was published and distributed something new would appear that I would want you to have. If possible, I will add each purchaser to my database. Then, through emails or electronic newsletters, you will be provided with updated, current information.

Real estate syndication has been a good business for me and many others I know, and I wish you success.

Made in the USA
San Bernardino, CA
20 January 2017